PassKey EA Review
Part 3: Representation

IRS Enrolled Agent Exam
Study Guide 2013-2014 Edition

Authors:

Collette Szymborski, CPA

Richard Gramkow, EA

Christy Pinheiro, EA ABA®

Recent Praise for the PassKey EA Review Series

Kari Hutchens (Canon City, Colorado)
I passed all three exams with the cheapest study materials out there! Easy to understand and comprehensive. Even from Part 1 of the book (Individuals), I learned so much that I am going to amend two prior year tax returns and get over $1,000 back. Passing all three parts of the EA exam on the first try and getting some extra cash in my pocket gets this book an A+!

Ken Smith (Chicago, Illinois)
I studied like crazy, night and day, and passed all three parts of the EA exam in just eight days. And I passed on the first try!

Michael Mirth (North Las Vegas, Nevada)
I am happy to say I am now an enrolled agent. This was the only source I used to study besides some extra practice tests. The way the book presented the materials made it easy to comprehend. If you are looking for a detailed study guide, this one is for you.

Oliver Douglass
I found this book to be the least expensive and the best guide around. The tests are on the money and the explanations are so easy to comprehend. Thanks for a great book.

Baiye Zebulone
Great books. Straight to the point, and very good examples for SEE preparations. I used all three parts to prepare for the SEE and passed Parts 1 and 3 on the first sitting and Part 2 on the second sitting. I will recommend it to anybody who wants to pass the rigorous EA examination.

Carl Ganster (Wyomissing, Pennsylvania)
I passed all my tests on the first try in five months using the PassKey books. Every topic is covered. It is easy reading, with plenty of examples. I have recommended the books to others who have to take the test. Thanks, PassKey, for writing great test guides. So many of the ones out there are hard to understand.

Do you want to test yourself?
Then get the PassKey EA Exam Workbook, newly expanded for tax year 2012!

PassKey EA Review Workbook:
Six Complete Enrolled Agent Practice Exams

Thoroughly revised and updated for tax year 2012, this workbook features **six complete** enrolled agent practice exams, with detailed answers, to accompany the PassKey EA Review study guides. This workbook includes two full exams for each of the three parts of the EA exam: Individuals, Businesses, and Representation.

You can learn by testing yourself on 600 questions, with all of the answers clearly explained in the back of the book.

Test yourself, time yourself, and learn!

Editor: Cynthia Willett Sherwood, EA, MSJ

PassKey EA Review, Part 3: Representation, IRS Enrolled Agent Exam Study Guide 2013-2014 Edition

ISBN: 978-1-935664-24-6

First Printing. PassKey EA Review
PassKey EA Review® is a U.S. Registered Trademark

PassKey Publications, PO Box 580465, Elk Grove, CA 95758

www.PassKeyPublications.com

Part 3: Representation

Tammy the Tax Lady ®

It's just easier this way... he's always in my pocket anyway!

Table of Contents

Introduction

Congratulations on taking the first step toward becoming an enrolled agent, a widely respected professional tax designation. The Internal Revenue Service licenses enrolled agents, known as EAs, after candidates pass a three-part exam testing their knowledge of federal tax law.

This PassKey study guide is designed to help you study for the EA exam, which is formally called the *IRS Special Enrollment Examination* or *"SEE."* The exam covers all aspects of federal tax law, including the taxation of individuals; corporations, partnerships, and exempt entities; ethics; and IRS collection and audit procedures. This guide is designed for the 2013 to 2014 testing season, which begins May 1, 2013 and closes February 28, 2014. Anyone taking the EA exam during this time period will be tested on 2012 tax law.

Exam Basics

The EA exam consists of three parts, which candidates typically take on different dates that do not need to be consecutive. The exam is exclusively administered by the testing company Prometric. You can find valuable information and register online at: ***http://www.prometric.com/IRS***

The yearly pass rates for the SEE vary by exam. In the 2011-2012 testing period, an average of more than 80% of test-takers passed Parts 1 and 3. The pass rate for Part 2 was much lower, averaging about 60%.

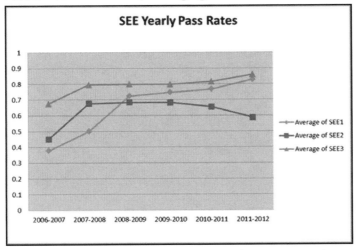

The computerized exam is offered only at Prometric testing centers. The format is multiple choice, with no questions requiring written answers. The length of each part of the exam is 3.5 hours, not including a pre-exam tutorial and post-exam survey.

Testing Center Procedures

The testing center is designed to be a secure environment. The following are procedures you'll need to follow on test day:

1. Check in about a half-hour before your appointment time, and bring a current government-issued ID with both a photo and signature. If you don't have valid ID, you'll be turned away and you'll have to pay for a new exam appointment.
2. You'll be given a locker for your wallet, phone, and other personal items. You won't be able to bring any reference materials or other items into the testing room, with the exception of soft earplugs. The center supplies noise-blocking headphones.
3. No food, water, or other beverages are allowed in the testing room.
4. You'll be given scratch paper and a pencil to use, which will be collected after the exam.
5. You'll be able to use an onscreen calculator during the exam, or Prometric will provide you with a handheld calculator. You cannot bring your own.
6. Before going into the testing room, you'll be scanned with a metal detector wand.
7. You'll need to sign in and out every time you leave the testing room. Bathroom breaks are permitted, but the test timer will continue to count down.
8. You're not allowed to talk or communicate with other test-takers in the exam room. Prometric continuously monitors the testing via video, physical walk-throughs, and an observation window.

Violation of any of these procedures may result in the disqualification of your exam. In cases of cheating, the IRS says candidates may be subject to a variety of consequences, including civil and criminal penalties.

Exam-takers who require special accommodations under the Americans with Disabilities Act (ADA) must contact Prometric at 888-226-9406 to obtain an accommodation request form. A language barrier is not considered a disability. [1]

---

[1] *Candidate Information Bulletin* for the Enrolled Agent Special Enrollment Examination.

Exam Content

The IRS introduces multiple versions of new EA exams each May. If you fail a particular part of the exam and need to retake it, don't expect to see the identical questions the next time.

The IRS no longer releases new test questions and answers, although questions from 2003 to 2005 are available on the IRS website for review. (Be aware that tax law changes every year, so make sure you are familiar with recent updates and don't rely too heavily on these sample questions and answers.) Prometric includes broad exam content outlines for each exam part; however, not all of the topics will appear on the exam and there may be other topics that are included.

Your PassKey study guides present an overview of all the major areas of federal taxation that enrolled agents typically encounter in their practices and that are likely to appear on the exam. Although the PassKey guides are designed to be comprehensive, we suggest you review IRS publications and try to learn as much as you can about tax law in general so that you're well-equipped to take the exam. In addition to this study guide, we highly recommend that all exam candidates read:

- **Publication 17, *Your Federal Income Tax*** (for Part 1 of the exam), and
- **Circular 230, *Regulations Governing the Practice of Attorneys, Certified Public Accountants, Enrolled Agents, Enrolled Actuaries, and Appraisers before the Internal Revenue Service*** (for Part 3 of the exam).

Anyone may download these publications for free from the IRS website.

> **Note:** Some exam candidates take Part 3, *Representation, Practice, and Procedures,* first, rather than taking the tests in order, since the material in Part 3 is considered less complex. The IRS discourages taking the tests out of order by including multiple questions (5% or more at times) of material that relates to taxation of *Individuals* and *Businesses.*

Exam Strategy

Each multiple choice question provides four choices for an answer. There are several different multiple choice formats used:[2]

---

[2] Candidate Information Bulletin for the Enrolled Agent Special Enrollment Examination.

Format One- Direct Question

Which of the following entities are required to file Form 709, United States Gift Tax Return?

A. An individual
B. An estate or trust
C. A corporation
D. All of the above

Format Two-Incomplete sentence

Supplemental wages are compensation paid in addition to an employee's regular wages. They **do not** include payments for_____.

A. Accumulated sick leave
B. Nondeductible moving expenses
C. Vacation pay
D. Travel reimbursements paid at the federal government per diem rate

---

Format Three-All of the following EXCEPT

There are five tests which must be met for you to claim an exemption for a dependent. Which of the following is **not** a requirement?

A. Citizen or Resident Test
B. Member of Household or Relationship Test
C. Disability Test
D. Joint Return Test

There may also be a limited number of questions on the exam that have four choices, with three of them incorrect statements or facts and only one that is a correct statement or fact, which you would select as the right answer.[3] All four of these question-and-answer formats appear in your PassKey study guides. During the EA exam, you need to make sure you read each question thoroughly to understand exactly what is being asked.

Your exam may also include some experimental questions that will not be scored. You won't know which ones they are—the IRS uses them to gather statistical information on the questions before they're added to the exam as scored items.

---

[3] 1-31-13: Telephone interview with Larry Orozco, IRS director of competency and standards.

To familiarize yourself with the computerized testing format, there's a tutorial on the Prometric website. If you're not sure of an answer, you may mark it for review and return to it later. Try to eliminate clearly wrong answers of the four possible choices to narrow your odds of selecting the right answer. But be sure to answer every question, even if you have to guess, because all answers left incomplete will be marked as incorrect. Each question is weighted equally.

In the 3.5 hours of the exam, you'll have 210 minutes to answer questions, or slightly more than two minutes per question. Try to answer the questions you're sure about quickly, so you can devote more time to those that include calculations or that you're not as sure about. Remember that the clock doesn't stop for bathroom breaks, so try to allocate your time wisely.

Scoring

After you finish your exam and submit your answers, you'll learn immediately from a Prometric staff member whether you passed or failed. In either case, you won't receive a printout of the questions you answered correctly or missed.

The IRS determines scaled scores by calculating the number of questions answered correctly from the total number of questions in the examination and converting to a scale that ranges from 40 to 130. The IRS has set the scaled passing score at 105, which corresponds to the minimum level of knowledge deemed acceptable for EAs. Under its testing system, the IRS does not release the percentage of questions that you need to answer correctly in order to pass.

If you pass, you'll receive a score report showing a passing designation, but not your actual score. The IRS considers all candidates who pass as qualified, but does not rank *how* qualified each person may be.

If you fail, you'll receive a scaled score between 40 and 104, so you'll be able to see how close you are to the minimum score of 105. You'll also receive diagnostic information to help you know subject areas you need to focus on when retaking the exam:

- 1: Area of weakness where additional study is necessary. It is important for you to focus on this domain as you prepare to take the test again. You may want to consider taking a course or participating actively in a study group on this topic.
- 2: May need additional study.

- 3: Clearly demonstrated an understanding of subject area.[4]

If necessary, you may take each part of the exam up to four times during the May 1 and February 28 testing window. You'll need to re-register with Prometric and pay fees for each new time you take an exam part.

You can carry over passing scores for individual parts of the exam up to two years from the date you took them.

After Passing

Once you've passed the exam, you must apply for enrollment as an EA, which includes an IRS review of your tax compliance history. Failure to timely file or pay personal income taxes can be grounds for denial of enrollment. You may not practice as an EA until the IRS approves your application and issues you a Treasury Card.

Successfully passing the EA exam can launch you into a fulfilling and lucrative new career. The exam requires intense preparation and diligence, but with the help of Passkey's comprehensive *EA Review*, you'll have the tools you need to learn how to become an enrolled agent.

We wish you much success.

---

[4] *Candidate Information Bulletin* for the Enrolled Agent Special Enrollment Examination.

Ten Steps for the IRS EA Exam

STEP 1-Learn

Learn more about the enrolled agent designation and explore the career opportunities that await you after passing your three-part EA exam. In addition to preparing taxes for individuals and businesses, EAs can represent people before the IRS, just like attorneys and CPAs. Many people who use the PassKey study guides have had no previous experience in preparing taxes, but go on to rewarding new professional careers.

STEP 2-Gather information

Gather more information before you launch into your studies. The IRS publishes basic information about becoming an EA on its website at www.irs.gov/Tax-Professionals/Enrolled-Agents. You'll also find valuable information about the exam itself on the Prometric testing website at www.prometric.com/see. Be sure to download the *Candidate Information Bulletin*, which takes you step-by-step through the registration and testing process.

STEP 3-Obtain a PTIN

A PTIN stands for "Preparer Tax Identification Number." Before you can register for your EA exam, you must obtain a PTIN, which is issued by the IRS.[5] The sign-up system can be found at www.irs.gov/ptin. You'll need to create an account, complete an on-line application, and pay a required fee.

STEP 4-Sign up with Prometric

Once you have your PTIN, you may register for your exam on the Prometric website. After creating an account and paying the required testing fee, you can complete the registration process by clicking on "Scheduling."

STEP 5-Schedule a time, date, and location

You'll be able to choose a test site and time and date that are convenient for you. Prometric has test centers in most major metropolitan areas of the United States, as well as certain other parts of the world. You may schedule as little as two days in advance—space permitting—through the website or by calling 800-306-

---

[5] Foreign-based candidates do not need a PTIN to register to take the exam.

3926 Monday through Friday. Be aware that the website and the phone line have different inventory of available times and dates, so you may want to check the other source if your preferred date is already full.

STEP 6-Adopt a study plan

Focus on one exam part at a time, and adopt a study plan that covers all the tax topics on the EA exam. You'll need to develop an individualized study program based on your current level of tax knowledge. For those without prior tax experience, a good rule of thumb is to study at least 60 hours for each of the three exam sections, committing at least 15 hours per week. Start well in advance of the exam date.

STEP 7-Get plenty of rest, exercise, and good nutrition

Get plenty of rest, exercise, and good nutrition prior to the EA exam. You'll want to be at your best on exam day.

STEP 8-Test day has arrived!

On test day, make sure you remember your government-issued ID and arrive early at the test site. Prometric advises to arrive at least 30 minutes before your scheduled examination time. If you miss your appointment and are not allowed to test, you'll forfeit your exam fee and have to pay for a new appointment.

STEP 9-During the exam

This is when your hard work finally pays off. Focus, don't worry if you don't know every question, but make sure you allocate your time appropriately. Give your best answer to every question. All questions left blank will be marked as wrong.

Step 10-Congratulations. You passed!

After celebrating your success, you need to apply for your EA designation. The quickest way is by filling out Form 23, *Application for Enrollment to Practice Before the Internal Revenue Service*, directly on the IRS website. Once your application is approved, you'll be issued a Treasury card, and you'll be official—a brand new enrolled agent!

New Tax Preparer Information For 2012
Part 3: Representation

RTRP Program Suspended: On January 18, 2013, the U.S. District Court for the District of Columbia directed the IRS to stop enforcing the requirements for registered tax return preparers. In accordance with this order, RTRPs are not required to complete competency testing or secure continuing education. This ruling does not affect the practice requirements for other enrolled practitioners (CPAs, attorneys, enrolled agents, enrolled retirement plan agents, or enrolled actuaries). The IRS has stated that they plan to appeal this decision.[6]

Mandatory PTIN Requirement: Beginning in 2011 all paid preparers were required to have a Preparer Tax Identification Number (PTIN) *before* preparing returns. The mandatory PTIN requirement was suspended for a short time due to pending litigation, and was reinstated February 1, 2013.

PTIN Helpline: PTIN applicants can obtain (and renew) their PTIN online using the IRS website (www.irs.gov/ptin). The fee is $64.25. The PTIN helpline is 1-877-613-7846.

OPR Mailbox Suspended: Effective in 2012, the former OPR e-mail address is no longer in operation. This is because many preparers were receiving fraudulent e-mails that purported to be from the Office of Professional Responsibility.

Reporting Preparer Violations: Starting in 2012, taxpayers are able to report tax preparers in violation of Circular 230 guidelines using the new Form 14157, *Complaint: Tax Return Preparer*. This form is appropriate for reporting violations of both enrolled and unenrolled preparers.

TAC Refusing Bulk Returns: Starting in 2012, IRS offices will no longer accept bulk returns for processing. The IRS wants to eliminate the practice of tax preparers dropping off completed returns for processing, especially during peak operating periods. However, TACs will still accept returns with imminent statute implications, with remittances or other time-sensitive situations.

ITIN/SSN Mismatch: For tax year 2012, it is now possible to e-file returns with an ITIN/SSN mismatch. The IRS made this change on June 22, 2012.

---

[6] Sabina Loving, et. al. v. Internal Revenue Service

ITIN Application Requirements Changed: Starting in 2012, Forms W-7, *Application for IRS Individual Taxpayer Identification Number*, must include **original** documentation such as passports and birth certificates. Notarized copies or photocopies of documentation are no longer sufficient.

Stockpiling: The IRS announced on January 4, 2013 that the stockpiling of 2012 returns is allowed. The Internal Revenue Service temporarily lifted its prohibition against stockpiling tax returns before e-filing due to the late tax law changes.[7]

---

[7] The American Taxpayer Relief Act of 2012, better known as the "fiscal cliff" legislation.

Unit 1: Rules Governing Authority to Practice

> **More Reading:**
> Circular 230, *Regulations Governing the Practice of Attorneys, Certified Public Accountants, Enrolled Agents, Enrolled Actuaries, Enrolled Retirement Plan Agents, and Appraisers Before the Internal Revenue Service*
> Publication 947, *Practice Before the IRS and Power of Attorney*
> Publication 470, *Limited Practice Without Enrollment*

Overview of Part 3: Representation, Practice, and Procedures

Part 3 of the EA exam concerns the ethics and laws that regulate the tax profession: who is allowed to prepare taxes for compensation; who may represent taxpayers in appeals hearings before the IRS; what standards the tax profession is held to; what IRS procedures must be followed when it comes to assessing and collecting taxes; what rules guide the IRS in conducting audits; and what penalties tax preparers who violate the law face.

These issues and more are dealt with in detail in Treasury Department Circular No. 230,[8] which underwent a sweeping revision in 2011. The update of Circular 230 is part of a series of steps designed to increase oversight of federal tax return preparation. All enrolled practitioners[9] who represent taxpayers before the IRS are subject to the rules and regulations set forth in Circular 230.

"Practice before the IRS"

"Practice before the IRS" includes all matters connected with a presentation before the IRS, or any issues relating to a client's rights, privileges, or liabilities under laws or regulations administered by the IRS. "Practice before the IRS" is currently defined as:

- Communicating with the IRS on behalf of a taxpayer regarding his rights, privileges, or liabilities under laws and regulations administered by the IRS
- Representing a taxpayer at conferences, hearings, or meetings with the IRS
- Preparing and filing documents, including tax returns, for the IRS
- Corresponding and communicating with the IRS for a taxpayer

---

[8]Regulations governing practice are set forth in Title 31, Code of Federal Regulations, Subtitle A, Part 10, and are published in pamphlet form as Treasury Department Circular No. 230 on June 3, 2011.
[9] An "enrolled practitioner" is simply a tax professional who is allowed to represent taxpayers before the IRS. Usually, this is an EA, CPA, or attorney. See the following section for a detailed explanation of enrolled practitioners and some narrow exceptions to this rule.

- Providing a client with written advice that has a potential for tax avoidance or evasion

> **Example:** Trina is a CPA. Her client, Samuel, has a large tax debt. Samuel does not wish to communicate directly with the IRS, but he wants to set up an installment agreement. Trina has Samuel sign Form 2848 giving her power of attorney and then she calls the IRS on his behalf and sets up the installment agreement for him. This action is considered "Practice before the IRS."

U.S. citizenship is not required to practice before the IRS, and, in fact, many EAs, CPAs and attorneys work abroad helping expatriate taxpayers with their U.S. tax returns while they are living overseas.

Actions That Are Not "Practice Before the IRS"

"Practice before the IRS" does NOT include:

- Representation of taxpayers before the U.S. Tax Court. The Tax Court has its own rules of practice and its own rules regarding admission to practice.
- Merely appearing as a witness for the taxpayer is not practice before the IRS. In general, individuals who are not "enrolled practitioners" may appear before the IRS as witnesses—but they *may not advocate* for the taxpayer.

Enrolled Practitioners (§10.3 Who May Practice Before the IRS)

The following individuals who are not currently under suspension or disbarment may represent taxpayers before the IRS by virtue of their licensing. There are also some other individuals who may practice before the IRS because of a "special relationship" with the taxpayer, explained later in this unit.

Attorneys

Any attorney who is a member in good standing of the bar may practice before the IRS in all fifty states. A *student attorney* may also practice before the IRS by virtue of his status as a law student under Section 10.7(d) of Circular 230.

Certified Public Accountants (CPAs)

Any CPA who is duly qualified may practice before the IRS in all fifty states. A *student CPA candidate* may also practice before the IRS by virtue of his status as a CPA student under Section 10.7(d) of Circular 230.

Enrolled Agents (EAs)

Any enrolled agent in active status may practice before the IRS. An EA is a person who has earned the privilege of representing taxpayers before the IRS in all fifty states. Like attorneys and CPAs, EAs are unrestricted as to which taxpayers they can represent, what types of tax matters they can handle, and which IRS offices they can represent clients before. EAs are allowed to represent taxpayers in the U.S. Tax Court only if they have passed the U.S. Tax Court exam.

Enrolled Actuaries (Limited Practice)

Any individual who is enrolled as an actuary by the Joint Board for the Enrollment of Actuaries may practice before the IRS. The practice of enrolled actuaries is limited to certain Internal Revenue Code sections that relate to their area of expertise, principally those sections governing employee retirement plans.

Enrolled Retirement Plan Agents (Limited Practice)

Similar to an EA, an enrolled retirement plan agent (ERPA) is allowed to practice before the IRS. However, an ERPA's practice is limited to certain Internal Revenue Code sections that relate to their area of expertise, principally those sections governing employee retirement plans.

Registered Tax Return Preparers (DESIGNATION UNDER SUSPENSION)

Under the terms of Circular 230, any individual *other than* an attorney, CPA, enrolled agent, enrolled actuary, or ERPA who prepares a tax return and signs it as a paid preparer must be a registered tax return preparer (RTRP).[10] This provision was part of the major changes made to Circular 230 in 2011. The IRS wanted anyone who prepared tax returns for compensation to pass an IRS competency test and be subject to annual continuing education requirements.

However, under the terms of a district court ruling in January 2013,[11] the IRS is blocked from enforcing the regulatory requirements for registered tax return preparers. The court found that the IRS "lacks statutory authority to promulgate or enforce the new regulatory scheme for 'registered tax return preparers' brought under Circular 230."

The court ruling means that the new RTRP designation is currently under suspension. The RTRP regulations had been expected to affect many thousands of

---

[10]Circular 230 §10.4(c).
[11] *Loving*, No. 12-385, U.S. District Court for the District of Columbia, 1/18/2013.

tax practitioners who prepare tax returns for a fee, without any professional certification, testing, or continuing education requirements.

The IRS has announced it plans to appeal the district court's ruling. In the meantime, as of publication, the RTRP competency test is not being offered for 2013. It is unclear whether the IRS will choose to, or be allowed to, offer the test on a voluntary basis only, or whether Congress will step in and grant the IRS broader authority to regulate tax preparers.

Volunteer Students at Tax Clinics

Students volunteering in a Low Income Taxpayer Clinic (LITC) or a Student Tax Clinic Program (STCP) may represent taxpayers before the IRS. A taxpayer also may authorize a volunteer with VITA, Volunteer Income Tax Assistance, to represent him before the IRS. Under VITA, volunteer tax preparers offer free tax help to taxpayers who make $51,000 or less and need help preparing their own tax returns.

Practice During Special Circumstances (§ 10.7 limited practice)

There are some exceptions to the general rule regarding enrolled practitioners (CPAs, EAs, and attorneys). Because of a "special relationship" with the taxpayer, certain individuals may represent some taxpayers before the IRS.

This "limited practice" rule usually applies to representatives for a business entity, such as an officer of a corporation. However, a family member may also "practice" before the IRS on behalf of another family member.

An individual (self-representation): Any individual may always represent *himself* before the IRS, provided he has appropriate identification (such as a driver's license or a passport). Even a disbarred individual may represent himself before the IRS.[12]

Example #1: Gary was a tax attorney who was disbarred because of a felony conviction in 2011. An individual who is disbarred is not eligible to represent taxpayers before the IRS. Gary was audited by the IRS in 2012. Despite being disbarred, Gary may still represent *himself* before the IRS during the examination of his own return.

---

[12] See § 10.7(a), Circular 230.

A family member: An individual family member may represent members of his immediate family. Family members include a spouse, child, parent, brother, or sister of the individual.

> **Example #2:** Emily is an accounting student who is not an enrolled practitioner. The IRS is auditing her brother. Emily is allowed to represent her brother before the IRS, meaning she can "practice before the IRS" in this limited circumstance. Because of the family relationship, Emily's brother is not required to be present during the examination (Circular 230 Section 10.7(c)(1)).

> **Example #3:** Jim's mother is being audited by the IRS. Even though Jim is not enrolled to practice before the IRS, he is allowed to represent his mother because of the family relationship.

An officer: A bona fide officer of a corporation (including parents, subsidiaries, or affiliated corporations) may represent the organization he is an officer of before the IRS.

A partner: A general partner may represent the partnership before the IRS. *Limited partners* in a partnership are considered merely investors and may not represent a partnership before the IRS.

An employee: A regular full-time employee can represent his employer. An employer can be an individual, partnership, corporation (including parents, subsidiaries, or affiliated corporations), association, trust, receivership, guardianship, estate, organized group, governmental unit, agency, or authority.

> **Example #4:** Angelique is a full-time bookkeeper for her employer. She is not an enrolled preparer. During the year, the IRS sent her employer a notice regarding some unfiled payroll tax returns. Angelique may file a Form 2848 and speak with the IRS on her employer's behalf because of the employee-employer relationship.

A fiduciary: A trustee, receiver, guardian, personal representative, administrator, or executor can represent the trust, receivership, guardianship, or estate. In the eyes of the IRS, a fiduciary is considered to be the taxpayer and not a representative of the taxpayer.

> **Example #5:** Tony was named the executor of his mother's estate after she passed away. He is not an enrolled preparer, but he is allowed to represent his mother's estate before the IRS. Tony is considered the *fiduciary* for the estate.

Authorization for Special Appearances: Only in very rare and compelling circumstances will the Commissioner of the IRS or a delegate authorize a person who is not otherwise eligible to practice before the IRS to represent another person for a particular matter.

Return Preparer Office

To better regulate preparers, the IRS has created a new department called the Return Preparer Office (RPO).

The RPO has oversight for all matters related to the authority to practice before the IRS, including:

- Taking action on registration applications for enrollment and renewal; administering competency testing; approving continuing education (CE) providers and accrediting organizations; and ensuring that CE requirements are met by practitioners or those seeking practitioner status.
- Making preliminary determinations regarding denial or termination of practitioner registration or enrollment; making preliminary determinations with respect to revocation of status for CE providers and accrediting organizations.
- Receiving and processing complaints regarding alleged preparer or practitioner misconduct; initiating preliminary investigations, including data gathering and referring complaints to the Office of Professional Responsibility, the Treasury Inspector General for Tax Administration, or the Criminal Investigation Division for further action.

The Office of Professional Responsibility (OPR) used to handle many of the functions that have been delegated to the RPO. The OPR is now primarily concerned with initiating disciplinary proceedings and determining sanctions related to practitioner misconduct.

Mandatory Tax Preparer Registration

Under the revised regulations of Circular 230, the IRS now requires the following:

- All paid tax return preparers must register with the IRS and obtain a Preparer Tax Identification Number (PTIN).
- Tax preparers who register will be subject to a limited tax compliance check to make sure that they have filed their own personal and business tax returns.

In addition, the IRS plans to require that all tax return preparers be subject to verification of personal and business tax compliance every three years.[13] These requirements only apply to tax preparers who prepare returns for compensation.

Exception for Supervised Preparers

Supervised preparers are individuals who do not sign tax returns as paid return preparers but are:

- Employed by a law firm, EA office, or CPA practice, and
- Are directly *supervised* by an attorney, CPA, EA, ERPA, or enrolled actuary who signs the returns prepared by the supervised preparer as the paid tax return preparer.

Supervised preparers may NOT:

- Sign any tax return they prepare or assist in preparing
- Represent taxpayers before the IRS in any capacity
- Identify themselves as a Circular 230 practitioner

When applying for or renewing a PTIN, supervised preparers must provide the PTIN of their supervisor.

Exception for Non-Form 1040 Series Preparers

Non-Form 1040 series preparers are individuals who do not prepare or assist in the preparation of any Form 1040 series tax return or claim for refund, except a Form 1040-PR or Form 1040-SS, for compensation. Both these forms are only for residents of Puerto Rico. Non-Form 1040 series preparers may sign tax returns they prepare or assist in preparing. They may also represent taxpayers before revenue agents, customer service representatives or similar officers and employees of the IRS during an examination, only if they signed the tax return that is being audited.

Mandatory IRS PTIN Requirement

In 2011, use of the PTIN became *mandatory* on all federal tax returns and claims for refund prepared by a paid tax preparer.[14] The PTIN is a nine-digit number that preparers must use when they prepare and sign a tax return or claim for re-

---

[13] IR-2010-1, Jan. 4, 2010.

[14] On February 1, 2013, the U.S. District Court for the District of Columbia modified its earlier court order to clarify that the injunction against registered tax return preparers does not affect the requirement for paid preparers to obtain PTINs. To comply with the earlier order of January 18, 2013, the IRS had suspended PTIN applications and renewals. It reactivated the system after the February 1 ruling.

fund. Previously, PTIN use was *optional* in place of the preparer's Social Security Number.

Multiple individuals cannot share one PTIN. A PTIN is assigned to a single preparer to identify that he or she is the preparer of a particular return.

Any preparer who is compensated for the preparation of (or *assists* in the preparation of) a tax return must apply for a PTIN. This includes attorneys, CPAs,[15] and EAs. Failure to obtain a PTIN could result in the imposition of Internal Revenue Code Section §6695 monetary penalties, injunction, and/or disciplinary action.

All tax preparers with existing PTINs are required to renew their PTINs online each year and pay a fee to do so. Preparers who fail to list a valid PTIN on tax returns they sign are subject to penalties of $50 per return, up to a maximum of $25,000 a year.

Persons Who Are Not Considered "Tax Preparers"

If there is no prior agreement for compensation, an individual who prepares a tax return is not considered an "income tax preparer" for IRS purposes. This is true even if the individual receives a gift or a favor in return. The agreement for compensation is the deciding factor as to whether or not a person is considered a "tax preparer" for IRS purposes.

Example: Terri is a retired CPA who only prepares tax returns for her close family members. She does not charge her family to prepare their tax returns. Sometimes, a family member will give Terri a gift in return. This year, she received home-baked cookies from her sister and a sweater from her niece. However, Terri does not ask for any gifts or expect them. She is not a "tax return preparer" for IRS purposes, and she is not required to obtain a PTIN.

Example: Bob is a retired tax professional. He does not have a PTIN. Bob volunteers during the tax filing season at a VITA site, where he prepares individual tax returns for lower-income individuals for free. Bob is not a "tax return preparer" and he is not required to have a PTIN.

An individual will not be considered an income "tax return preparer" in the following instances:

---

[15]Under the authority of Section 1.6109-2(h), attorneys and CPAs do not need to obtain a PTIN **unless** they prepare federal tax returns. All EAs are required to obtain PTINs.

- A person who merely gives an opinion about events that have not happened (such as tax advice for a business that has not been created).
- A person who merely furnishes typing, reproducing, or mechanical assistance.
- A person who merely prepares a return of his employer (or of an officer or employee of the employer) by whom the person is regularly and continuously employed.
- Any fiduciary who prepares a tax return for a trust or estate.[16]
- An unpaid volunteer who provides tax assistance under a VITA program.
- An unpaid volunteer who provides tax assistance in the Tax Counseling for the Elderly program.
- Any employee of the IRS who is performing official duties by preparing a tax return for a taxpayer who requests it.

Example: Thomas is a CPA. His neighbor, Ross, consults with Thomas about a business he is thinking about starting. Thomas gives Ross an opinion regarding the potential business and taxes. In this case, Thomas is not considered a "tax preparer" for the purpose of IRS preparer penalties. This is because Thomas is merely giving an opinion about events that have not happened yet.

Example: Ginny is a bookkeeper for Creative Candies Corporation. She is a full-time employee, and she prepares the payroll checks and payroll tax returns for all of the employees of Creative Candies. As a full-time employee, Ginny is not considered a "tax preparer" for the purpose of IRS regulations. Her employer is ultimately responsible for the accuracy of the payroll tax returns.

Example: Francisco is an EA who has a PTIN. He employs an administrative assistant, Claudia, who performs data entry during tax filing season. At times, clients call and provide Claudia with information, which she records in the system. Using the data she has entered, Francisco meets with his clients and provides tax advice as needed. He then prepares and signs their returns. Claudia is not a "tax return preparer" and is not required to have a PTIN.

Preparation of tax returns outside the U.S. is included in these rules. Tax preparers who work on U.S. tax returns overseas are still subject to Circular 230 regulations.

---

[16]Fiduciaries, as detailed by Section 7701(a)(36)(B)(iii) of the Internal Revenue Code, who file returns are not considered "tax return preparers" and are also not subject to the e-file mandate.

Employer of Tax Preparers

A tax preparer may employ other preparers. For example, if an enrolled agent owns a franchise that employs ten tax preparers, he or she, as the owner of the business, is the one who is primarily liable for any preparer penalties.

Any person who employs tax return preparers is required to retain records detailing the name, identifying number, and principal place of work of each income tax return preparer employed. The records of the income tax preparers must be made available upon request to the IRS. They must be retained and kept available for inspection for at least three years following the close of period for each tax return. The "return period" means the 12-month period beginning July 1 each year.

The "Substantial Portion" Rule

Only the person who prepares all or a substantial portion of a tax return shall be considered the "preparer" of the return. A person who merely gives advice on a portion or a single entry on the tax return is considered to have prepared only that portion. If more than one individual is involved in the preparation of a tax return, the preparer is the person with the primary responsibility for the overall accuracy of the return and must sign the return.

In order to identify who is responsible for a "substantial portion" of the return, the following guidelines may be used. A portion of a tax return is not typically considered to be "substantial" if it involves only minor dollar amounts of:

- Less than $2,000, or
- Less than 20% of the adjusted gross income on the return.

Usually, a single schedule would not be considered a "substantial portion" of a tax return, unless it represents a major portion of the income.

Example: Greg and Eli are partners in a tax practice. In March, Eli finishes a few returns that Greg had started before he left on vacation. Later, one tax return comes up for audit, and it is determined that the return has a gross misstatement. Greg prepared Schedule C on the return, and Eli prepared the rest of the return. Schedule C represents 95% of the income and expenses shown on the return. Therefore, for the purpose of any potential penalty, Greg is considered the "preparer" of this return, since he prepared the schedule that represents the majority of the income and expenses on the return.

Forms Used For Representation

There are three forms that are used for representation. The first is Form 2848, *Power of Attorney and Declaration of Representative*, which authorizes an individual to represent a taxpayer before the IRS. The individual authorized must be a person eligible to "practice before the IRS."

The next is Form 8821, *Tax Information Authorization*, which authorizes any individual, corporation, firm, organization or partnership to receive confidential information for the type of tax and the years or periods listed on the form.

The last is Form 56, *Notice Concerning Fiduciary Relationship*, to notify the IRS of the existence of a fiduciary relationship. A fiduciary (trustee, executor, administrator, receiver, or guardian) stands in the position of a taxpayer and technically acts as the taxpayer, not as a representative. Because the fiduciary stands in the position of the entity, the fiduciary signs the Form 56 on behalf of the entity.

IRS Power of Attorney and Disclosure Authorization

When a taxpayer wishes to use a representative, he must fill out and sign Form 2848, *Power of Attorney and Declaration of Representative.* This form authorizes another person to represent a taxpayer before the IRS. The representative must be eligible to practice before the IRS in order to complete Form 2848. If a tax professional is disbarred or suspended, his power of attorney will not be recognized by the IRS.

Only "natural persons" may practice before the IRS, which means that an entity such as a corporation or partnership is not eligible. Any person representing a taxpayer must be qualified, and the duty may not be delegated to an employee. An EA who fills out Form 2848 on behalf of a client must list his own name as the representative, rather than the name of his business.

Example #1: Caitlyn is an EA who operates Caitlyn Rivera's Accounting Corporation. When she prepares Form 2848 for a taxpayer, she must represent her client as an individual. Caitlyn is granted permission to represent her client, but her corporation is not.

A qualified representative can represent a taxpayer before the IRS *without* the taxpayer present, so long as the proper power of attorney is signed and submitted to the IRS. Any **authorized** representative can usually perform the following acts:

- Represent a taxpayer before any office of the IRS
- Record an interview or meeting with the IRS
- Sign an offer or a waiver of restriction on assessment or collection of a tax deficiency, or a waiver of notice of disallowance of claim for credit or refund
- Sign consents to extend the statutory time period for assessment or collection of a tax
- Sign a closing agreement
- Receive (but **never** endorse or cash) a tax refund check

A signed IRS Form 2848, *Power of Attorney and Declaration of Representative* (or other acceptable power of attorney, such as a durable power of attorney) is required in order for a tax professional to represent a taxpayer before the IRS.[17]

Form 2848 is used by:

- CPAs, enrolled agents, enrolled actuaries, and attorneys
- Other individuals, if specifically permitted, in limited circumstances (such as a family member representing a taxpayer, or an executor representing an estate)

A power of attorney is valid until revoked. It may be revoked by the taxpayer or revoked by the representative. A revocation statement must be submitted to the IRS in writing and must contain the taxpayer's identifying information, the representative's identifying information, and the specific tax and tax periods covered by the revocation. The statement should be signed and dated by the party desiring the revocation.

Example: Nicola is an EA. She had a power of attorney on file for her former client, Edwin. Nicola fired Edwin for nonpayment, but she continued to receive IRS notices on his behalf. Nicola prepares a revocation statement and submits it to the IRS, notifying the IRS that she no longer represents Edwin.

A power of attorney is generally terminated if the taxpayer becomes incapacitated or incompetent. A power of attorney is automatically rescinded when a new-

---

[17]A signed Form 2848 is not required when a taxpayer is deceased and is being represented by a fiduciary or executor.

er power of attorney is filed, *unless* the taxpayer *specifically requests* that the old power of attorney remain active.

A newly filed power of attorney concerning the same matter will revoke a previously filed power of attorney. For example, if a taxpayer changes preparers and the second preparer files a power of attorney on behalf of the taxpayer, the old power of attorney on file will be rescinded.

Non-IRS Powers of Attorney (Durable Power of Attorney)

The IRS will accept a non-IRS power of attorney (such as a durable power of attorney[18]), but it must contain all of the information present on a standard IRS Form 2848. If a practitioner wants to use a different power of attorney document other than Form 2848, it must contain the following information:

- The taxpayer's name, mailing address, and Social Security Number.
- The name and mailing address of the representative.
- The types of tax involved and the tax form number in question.
- The specific periods or tax years involved.
- For estate tax matters, the decedent's date of death.
- A clear expression of the taxpayer's intention concerning the scope of authority granted to the representative.
- The taxpayer's signature and date. The taxpayer must also attach to the non-IRS power of attorney a signed and dated statement made by the representative.

Example: Ronald signs a durable power of attorney that names his neighbor, Erik, as his attorney-in-fact.[19] The durable power of attorney grants Erik the authority to perform all acts on Ronald's behalf. However, it does not list specific tax-related information such as types of tax or tax form numbers. Shortly after Ronald signs the power of attorney, he is declared incompetent. Later, a tax matter arises concerning a prior year return filed by Ronald. Erik attempts to represent Ronald before the IRS, but is rejected because the durable power of attorney does not contain required information. If Erik attaches a statement (signed under the penalty of perjury) that the durable power of attorney is valid under the laws of the governing jurisdiction, he can sign a completed Form 2848 and submit it on Ronald's behalf. If Erik can practice before the IRS, he can name himself as the representative on Form 2848.

---

[18] Durable power of attorney: A power of attorney that is not subject to a time limit and that will continue in force after the incapacitation or incompetency of the taxpayer.

[19] Attorney-in-fact: A person who holds power of attorney and therefore is legally designated to transact business and other duties on behalf of another individual.

IRS Form 8821, Disclosure Authorization

Form 8821, *Tax Information Authorization* (TIA), authorizes any individual, corporation, firm, organization, or partnership to receive confidential information for the type of tax and periods listed on Form 8821. Any third party may be designated to receive tax information.

IRS Form 8821 is used by tax preparers, banks, employers, and other institutions to receive financial information on behalf of an individual or a business.

Form 8821 is only a disclosure form, so it will not give an individual any power to represent a taxpayer before the IRS. Form 8821 only may be used to obtain information, such as copies of tax returns.

Representative Signing in Lieu of the Taxpayer

A representative named under a power of attorney is generally not permitted to sign a personal income tax return unless BOTH of the following are true:

- The signature is permitted under the Internal Revenue Code and the related regulations.
- The taxpayer specifically permits signature authority on the power of attorney.

For example, IRS regulations permit a representative to sign a taxpayer's return if the taxpayer is unable to sign for any of the following reasons:

- Disease or injury (for example, a taxpayer who is completely paralyzed or who has a debilitating injury)
- Continuous absence from the United States (including Puerto Rico) for a period of at least 60 days prior to the date required by law for filing the return
- Other good cause if specific permission is requested of and granted by the IRS

> **Example:** Geoffrey is an EA. He has a client named Sally who travels extensively for business. Sally has signed Form 2848 specifically granting Geoffrey the right to sign her tax returns in her absence. Sally is currently traveling outside the U.S. for business and will not return until four months after the due date of her returns. Geoffrey is allowed to sign Sally's return (Publication 947).

When a tax return is signed by a representative, it must be accompanied by a power of attorney authorizing the representative to sign the return.[20]

Spousal Signatures: Exceptions

In the case of a joint return, both spouses must agree to sign the return. However, there are special circumstances in which a spouse may sign on behalf of the other spouse. One spouse can sign the return on the other spouse's behalf, **without** a power of attorney, in the following instances:

- Because of a medical or physical condition that makes the spouse unable to sign the return.
- If one spouse is mentally incompetent, the other may sign the return as a guardian.
- If one spouse is serving in a combat zone (or serving in a combat zone in "missing" status), the other spouse can still file a joint return and sign it. A joint return filed under these circumstances is valid even if it is later determined that the missing spouse died before the year covered by the return.

In any other circumstance, a spouse may sign for another spouse, but a valid power of attorney would be required.

In the case of a minor child, the parent or legal guardian may sign the return by signing the child's name, followed by guardian's signature and their relationship to the child, (such as "parent" or "guardian for minor child"). A parent or guardian does not need a power of attorney in order to sign on behalf of a minor child.

The Centralized Authorization File (CAF)

A Centralized Authorization File, or "CAF," is the IRS's computer database that contains information regarding the type of authorization that taxpayers have given representatives for their accounts.

When a practitioner submits a power of attorney document to the IRS, it is processed for inclusion in the CAF. A CAF number is assigned to a tax practitioner or other authorized individual when a Form 2848 or Form 8821 is filed.

---

[20] Regulations Section 1.6012-1(a)(5)

Example: Josie is not a tax return preparer. In 2011, Josie's son, David, is audited by the IRS. David is 21 years old and does not wish to speak directly with the IRS. Josie files a Form 2848 and becomes the "authorized representative" for her son. She is issued a CAF number.

The issuance of a CAF number does not indicate that a person is either recognized or authorized to practice before the IRS. It merely confirms that a centralized file for authorizations has been established for the representative under that number.

Example: Darren is an EA who recently submitted Form 2848 to the IRS on behalf of his client, Jennifer. He later called the IRS to check the status of Jennifer's tax refund. The IRS employee requested Darren's CAF number, which he provided. The IRS employee found Jennifer's power of attorney information in the CAF system and gave Darren the information about his client's refund.

A CAF number also enables the IRS to automatically send copies of notices and other IRS communications to a representative.

Summary of Tax Return Preparer Requirements

Quick Reference

Type of Preparer	PTIN	IRS Test	Continuing Education	Practice Rights
Enrolled Agent (EA)	Yes	Yes (EA exam)	72 hours every 3 years (16 hours and 2 hours of ethics per year)	Unlimited
Certified Public Accountant (CPA)	Yes	No	Varies by state	Unlimited
Attorney	Yes	No	Varies by state	Unlimited
Supervised Preparer	Yes	No	No	Limited

Unit 1: Questions

1. For taxpayers who want someone to represent them in their absence at an examination with the IRS, all of the following statements are correct except:

A. The taxpayer must furnish that representative with written authorization on Form 2848, *Power of Attorney and Declaration of Representative*, or any other properly written authorization.
B. The representative can be an attorney, CPA, or EA.
C. The representative can be any person who helped the taxpayer prepare the return.
D. Even if the taxpayer appointed a representative, the taxpayer may choose to attend the examination or appeals conference and may act on his own behalf.

The answer is C. Only certain persons are allowed to represent a taxpayer before the IRS. Usually, only an attorney, CPA, or EA may represent a taxpayer before the IRS without the taxpayer present. ###

2. Which of the following individuals does not qualify as an enrolled practitioner under Circular 230?

A. Certified public accountant.
B. Enrolled actuary.
C. Unenrolled student volunteer at a VITA site.
D. All of the above are considered enrolled practitioners.

The answer is D. All of the practitioners listed qualify to represent a taxpayer before the IRS, under certain circumstances. Student volunteers at a VITA site are given a special exemption to represent taxpayers before the IRS. VITA is the IRS's Volunteer Income Tax Assistance program, designed to help low-income taxpayers. ####

3. In order to practice before the IRS, attorneys and CPAs licensed to practice in a particular state must _____:

A. Be in good standing in that state and may practice before the IRS only in that state.
B. Be in good standing in that state and may practice before the IRS in any state.
C. Take the EA exam in order to practice outside the state in which they are licensed.
D. None of the above.

The answer is B. Any attorney or certified public accountant who is not currently under suspension or disbarment from practice before the IRS and who is licensed in good standing in any state, possession, territory, commonwealth, or the District of Columbia may practice before the IRS. Enrolled agents may practice in any state. ###

4. Which of the following statements is true?

A. A parent has authority to represent her child before the IRS only if the child is a minor.
B. A parent has authority to represent her child before the IRS without the child present.
C. A parent cannot represent her child before the IRS without an enrolled practitioner present.
D. None of the above.

The answer is B. A parent may represent her child before the IRS. The child is not required to be at the examination. A family member may represent, without compensation, a taxpayer before the IRS. ###

5. Denise and Gabriela are best friends. They are not family members. Gabriela must appear before the IRS for an examination. Denise wants to appear before the IRS on her best friend's behalf, though she is not an enrolled preparer. Which of the following statements is true?

A. Denise may represent Gabriela before the IRS without Gabriela being present.
B. Denise may advocate for Gabriela to the best of her ability.
C. Denise may appear before the IRS as a witness and communicate information.
D. Denise may not appear before the IRS in any capacity.

The answer is C. Simply appearing as a witness before the IRS is allowed and not considered "practice before the IRS." Individuals who are not practitioners may appear before the IRS as witnesses or communicate to the IRS on a taxpayer's behalf—but they may not advocate for the taxpayer. ###

6. Which of the following individuals is required to obtain a PTIN?

A. A CPA who does not prepare any tax returns.
B. An EA who works for a CPA firm, but does not sign any tax returns.
C. A tax attorney who only does representation before the Supreme Court.
D. A retired accountant who prepares tax returns for free for his family.

The answer is B. All EAs are required to obtain PTINs as a condition of their licensing (the PTIN must be included on Form 23, which is the application form to become an enrolled agent). Attorneys and CPAs do not need to obtain a PTIN unless they prepare tax returns for compensation. Someone who prepares returns for free is not considered a "tax return preparer" by the IRS and does not need a PTIN. ###

7. Matthew is a full-time employee for Parkway Partnership. He is not an EA, attorney, or CPA. Parkway requests that Matthew represent the partnership in connection with an IRS audit. Which of the following statements is true?

A. Matthew is allowed to represent the partnership before the IRS.
B. Matthew is not allowed to represent the partnership before the IRS.
C. Matthew is only allowed to represent individual partners before the IRS.
D. None of the above.

The answer is A. Matthew is a full-time employee for Parkway Partnership, so in that capacity he may represent his employer before the IRS. A regular full-time employee of an individual employer may represent the employer (Circular 230, §10.7). ###

8. Which of the following parties is allowed to act as an official representative for a taxpayer before the IRS?

A. An unenrolled tax practitioner who did not prepare the tax return in question.
B. A taxpayer's neighbor who is not a CPA, attorney, or EA.
C. A limited partner in a partnership.
D. A student attorney.

The answer is D. A student attorney who receives permission to practice before the IRS by virtue of his status as a law student under Section 10.7(d) of Circular 230 is allowed to practice before the IRS. ###

9. Barry helps his friend, José, who does not speak English fluently. Barry appears before the IRS and translates for José at an IRS examination. Which of the following is true?

A. Barry is practicing before the IRS.
B. José must sign Form 2848 authorizing Barry to represent him.
C. Barry is not considered to be "practicing before the IRS."
D. The IRS prohibits unrelated persons from being present at an IRS examination.

The answer is C. Simply appearing as a witness or communicating information to the IRS does not constitute "practice before the IRS." Barry is merely assisting with the exchange of information and is not advocating on Jose's behalf. An example of an individual assisting with information exchange but not practicing would be a taxpayer's friend serving as a translator when the taxpayer does not speak English (IRS Manual Chapter 25). ###

10. A Centralized Authorization File (CAF) is _____.

A. An IRS computer file with information regarding the authority of an individual appointed under a power of attorney or person designated under a tax information authorization.
B. A file containing a practitioner's own personal tax return files, in order to assist with compliance regulation and monitoring of enrolled individuals.
C. An automated list of disbarred tax preparers.
D. An automated file of taxpayer delinquencies.

The answer is A. The CAF contains information on third parties authorized to represent taxpayers before the IRS and/or receive and inspect confidential tax information on active tax accounts or those accounts currently under consideration by the IRS. ###

11. Which of the following is considered a "paid preparer" under the Circular 230 regulations?

A. A full-time bookkeeper working for an employer who prepares payroll tax returns.
B. A retired attorney who prepares tax returns under the VITA program.
C. A person who merely furnishes typing, reproducing, or mechanical assistance.
D. A full-time secretary who also prepares tax returns for pay part-time from home during tax season.

The answer is D. A person who prepares tax returns for compensation is a paid preparer, even if the activity is only part-time. A person who prepares and signs a tax return WITHOUT compensation (such as for a family member or as a volunteer) is not considered a tax return preparer for the purposes of the preparer penalties. An employee who prepares a tax return for his employer or for another employee is not a "preparer" under Circular 230. The employer (or the individual with supervisory responsibility) has the responsibility for accuracy of the return. ####

12. How long is a power of attorney authorization valid?

A. One year.
B. Three years.
C. Until it is revoked or superseded.
D. Until the due date of the next tax return.

The answer is C. A power of attorney is valid until revoked or superseded. It may be revoked by the taxpayer or withdrawn by the representative, or it may be superseded by the filing of a new power of attorney for the same tax and tax period. ###

13. "Practice before the IRS" does not include:

A. Communicating with the IRS on behalf of a taxpayer regarding his rights or liabilities.
B. Representing a taxpayer at conferences, hearings, or meetings with the IRS.
C. Preparing and filing documents for the IRS.
D. Representation of clients in the U.S. Tax Court.

The answer is D. Practice before the IRS does not include the representation of clients in the U.S. Tax Court. The Tax Court is independent of the IRS and has its own rules of practice and its own rules regarding admission to practice. ###

14. Khan is a CPA who employs Amy, an accounting student, to assist in the preparation of tax returns. Khan signs all of the tax returns. Which of the following statements is true?

A. Amy and Khan can share one PTIN.
B. Amy is required by law to sign the returns that she has prepared.
C. Amy is required to obtain a PTIN.
D. Amy cannot assist with the preparation of tax returns until she becomes a CPA.

The answer is C. Amy must obtain a PTIN. Every individual who, for compensation, prepares or assists in the preparation of a tax return or claim for refund must have his or her own PTIN. ###

15. Form 8821, *Tax Information Authorization*, may be used to authorize the following:

A. Any individual, corporation, firm, organization, or partnership to receive confidential information for the type of tax and periods listed on Form 8821.
B. Any designated third party to receive tax information.
C. Both A and B.
D. For unenrolled practitioners to indicate a representative relationship with a taxpayer and to authorize practice before the IRS.

The answer is C. Form 8821, *Tax Information Authorization*, authorizes any individual, corporation, firm, organization, or partnership to receive confidential information for the type of tax and periods listed on the form. Any third party may be designated by the taxpayer to receive confidential tax information. Form 8821 is only a disclosure form, so it will not give an individual any power to represent a taxpayer before the IRS. It may be used only to obtain information, such as copies of tax returns. ###

16. Willa is an EA with a signed Form 2848 from her client, who is currently under audit. Which of the following actions are not permitted?

A. Willa may record the audit meeting with the IRS examiner.
B. Willa may sign a consent to extend the statutory time period for assessment of tax.
C. Willa may receive and endorse a tax refund check on her client's behalf.
D. Willa may represent her client before the IRS appeals office, *without* the taxpayer present.

The answer is C. Form 2848 may be used by an enrolled tax practitioner to receive (but never endorse or cash) a refund check drawn on the U.S. Treasury. All of the other actions listed are permitted, so long as the tax practitioner is qualified to practice before the IRS. In this case, Willa is an enrolled agent, so her practice rights are unlimited. ###

17. Stan is an EA who already has a PTIN. What must he do to retain his existing PTIN?

A. Nothing extra is required after the initial application. Stan will be allowed to retain his PTIN so long as he is current in his enrollment status.
B. Stan must renew his PTIN every three years when he renews his enrollment status.
C. Stan cannot retain his existing PTIN. He must apply for a new PTIN every year.
D. Stan must renew his existing PTIN yearly, and a required fee must be paid.

The answer is D. The IRS now requires all paid preparers to have a Preparer Tax Identification Number (PTIN). Stan's PTIN must be renewed each year, and the required fee paid. Preparers must re-register using the new online system or Form W-12. In most cases, preparers will be issued the same PTIN, if they already have an existing PTIN. ###

18. Adele is a CPA with a bookkeeper, Ichiro, who assists in the preparation of returns. Ichiro has a PTIN and qualifies as a "supervised preparer" under Section 1.6109-2(h). He is not an EA or other enrolled practitioner. Ichiro may not:

A. Sign any tax return he prepares or assists in preparing.
B. Represent taxpayers before the IRS in any capacity.
C. Identify himself as a Circular 230 practitioner.
D. All of the above.

The answer is D. Supervised preparers may not:

- Sign any tax return they prepare or assist in preparing
- Represent taxpayers before the IRS in any capacity
- Identify themselves as Circular 230 practitioners

Individuals who apply for a PTIN under this provision are required to certify on their application that they are supervised by an attorney, CPA, or EA who signs the tax return. ###

19. What penalties can be imposed against tax return preparers who prepare tax returns for compensation, but refuse to obtain a PTIN?

A. None.
B. Censure by the IRS Office of Professional Responsibility.
C. Monetary penalties, injunction, and/or disciplinary action.
D. Automatic expulsion from the IRS e-file program.

The answer is C. Any individual who, for compensation, prepares or assists in the preparation of tax returns must have a PTIN. Failure to do so could result in the imposition of Internal Revenue Code Section 6695 monetary penalties, injunction, and/or disciplinary action. ###

20. Everett is an EA with a PTIN. His firm employs a bookkeeper named Fernanda. She gathers client receipts and invoices and organizes and records all information for Everett. Everett then uses the information that his bookkeeper has compiled and prepares all the tax returns. Which of the following statements is true?

A. Fernanda needs to have a PTIN, and she is required to become an EA because she assists in the preparation of returns.
B. Fernanda needs to have a PTIN, but she is not required to become an EA.
C. Fernanda is not a tax return preparer and is not required to have a PTIN.
D. None of the above.

The answer is C. Fernanda is not a tax return preparer and is not required to have a PTIN. An individual who provides only typing, reproduction, or other mechanical assistance, but does not actually prepare returns is not considered a "tax preparer" by the IRS. ###

21. A power of attorney may be revoked by _____.

A. The taxpayer.
B. The representative.
C. The U.S. Tax Court.
D. Both A and B.

The answer is D. A power of attorney may be revoked by the taxpayer or the representative. A revocation statement should be submitted in writing and must contain the taxpayer's identifying information, the representative's identifying information (name and CAF number), and the specific tax and tax periods covered by the revocation. ###

22. To determine which preparer is responsible for a "substantial portion" of a tax return, the following guidelines are used except:

A. Whoever has the primary responsibility for the accuracy of the return.
B. Whoever actually owns or manages the tax practice.
C. Whoever prepares the portion of the return that declares the greatest amount of adjusted gross income.
D. None of the above.

The answer is B. Ownership or management of a tax practice is immaterial in determining the substantial portion rule. The most important determination is whoever has the primary responsibility for the accuracy of the return. If several people are involving in preparing a return, the person who prepares the part of the return that declares the greatest amount of income would be considered the "preparer" who must sign the return. ###

23. Which of the following is considered a "preparer" under Circular 230?

A. An attorney that that does not prepare tax returns or give tax advice.
B. A reporting agent that occasionally provides paid consulting services on the issue of employee classification.
C. An employee who prepares his employer's federal tax returns
D. An employee of a tax preparation firm that collects receipts, organizes records, and collects information for an enrolled practitioner.

The answer is B. A reporting agent who renders tax advice to any client regarding employee classification, or any other tax issue, (for compensation) would be considered a "tax preparer" under Circular 230 (see Treasury Regulation section 301.7701-15(f)(6)). The new Circular 230 §10.2(a) expands the definition of practitioner to include any practitioner who prepares tax returns or provides tax advice for compensation. ###

24. Jay is a certified public accountant who specializes in audit work. He does not prepare tax returns, although he works for a CPA firm with a tax department. Is Jay required to obtain a PTIN?

A. No, he is not required to obtain a PTIN.
B. Yes, he is required to obtain a PTIN.
C. Jay is only required to obtain a PTIN if he is a full-time employee.
D. He is only required to obtain a PTIN if he is self-employed.

The answer is A. Jay is not required to obtain a PTIN. Attorneys and certified public accountants do not need to obtain a PTIN unless they prepare federal tax returns. ###

Unit 2: Rules of Enrollment

More Reading:
Publication 947, *Practice Before the IRS and Power of Attorney*

Initial Enrollment

Enrolled Agent Licensing

There are two tracks to become an enrolled agent, which are outlined in Circular 230. An individual may receive the designation by passing a three-part exam, or may become an EA by virtue of past employment with the IRS.[21]

Track I: Exam Track

For the first track, an EA candidate must apply for a PTIN and register to take the Special Enrollment Examination (SEE, also known as the "EA exam") with the testing company Prometric, by filling out Form 2587, *Application for Special Enrollment Examination*. An applicant must be at least 18 years old. A candidate then must do the following:

- Achieve passing scores on all three parts of the SEE.
- File Form 23 to apply for enrollment within one year of the date of passing the exam. The IRS says it takes about six weeks to process applications.
- Pass a background check conducted by the IRS. The tax compliance check makes sure the applicant has filed all necessary tax returns and has no outstanding tax liabilities. The suitability check determines whether an applicant has engaged in any conduct that would justify suspension or disbarment.

*Note: Do not confuse the form numbers. Applicants **apply** to take the EA exam by filing Form 2587, *Application for Special Enrollment Examination*. Candidates may also sign up online. Once the candidate passes all three parts of the EA exam, he must file Form 23, *Application for Enrollment to Practice before the Internal Revenue Service*, in order to obtain his Treasury card.

---

[21] The IRS may waive the requirement for former IRS employees to pass the EA and ERPA exams, but will not waive the requirement for the enrolled actuary exam.

Track II: Previous Experience with the IRS

For the second track, an EA candidate must possess a minimum of five years of past service with the IRS and technical experience as outlined in Circular 230. Application must be made within three years from the date the employee left the IRS. Factors considered with this second track are the length and scope of employment and the recommendation of the superior officer. The applicant then must:

- Apply for enrollment on Form 23.
- Pass a background check, which includes tax compliance and suitability check.

Former IRS employees who become enrolled agents without taking the EA exam may be granted limited or unlimited representation rights. The IRS's Return Preparer Office makes the determinations on applications for enrollment to practice.[22]

Denial of Enrollment

Any individual engaged in practice before the IRS who is involved in disreputable conduct is subject to disciplinary action or denial of enrollment.

Disreputable acts alone may be grounds for denial of enrollment, even after the candidate has passed the EA exam. Failure to timely file tax returns or to pay one's taxes may also be grounds for denying an application for enrollment. The Return Preparer Office must inform the applicant why he is denied an application for enrollment. If an applicant is denied enrollment, he may file a written appeal to the Office of Professional Responsibility within 30 days from the date of the notice. The appeal must be filed along with the candidate's reasoning why the enrollment application should be accepted.

Example: Todd passed all three parts of the EA exam in 2012. He properly filed Form 23 requesting enrollment. Because he had failed to file numerous tax returns in the past, his application was denied. Todd filed an appeal with the Office of Professional Responsibility, explaining that he had been seriously injured years ago and therefore had failed to file his tax returns on time. He attached proof of his reasoning, along with copies of medical bills and a letter from his doctor. Todd also showed that all his tax returns had been properly filed after his recovery. The OPR accepted Todd's appeal and granted him enrollment.

---

[22] Similar rules apply to the ERPA exam. The applicant must pass an exam or qualifying experience as a former IRS employee.

IRS Roster of Enrolled Agents and Enrolled Retirement Plan Agents

The Return Preparer Office maintains a roster of EAs and ERPAs. The roster includes enrolled individuals whose status is inactive or retired. The roster has the following information:

- Current enrolled agents:
  - Who have been granted enrollment to practice
  - Whose enrollment has been placed on inactive status for failure to meet the continuing education requirements for renewal of enrollment
- Inactive enrolled agents:
  - Whose status is inactive due to retirement
  - Whose offer of consent to resign from enrollment has been accepted by the OPR
- Other individuals (and employers, firms, or other entities, if applicable) censured, suspended, or disbarred from practice before the IRS or upon whom a monetary penalty was imposed
- Disqualified appraisers
- Enrolled retirement plan agents (ERPAs):
  - Who have been granted enrollment to practice
  - Whose enrollment has been placed on inactive status for failure to meet the continuing education requirements for renewal of enrollment

This roster is available for public inspection as authorized by the Secretary of the Treasury.

Renewal of Enrollment

Enrolled agents must renew their enrollment status every three years. If an EA does not renew his enrollment, he may not continue to practice as an enrolled agent. The three successive enrollment years preceding the effective date of renewal is referred to as the IRS enrollment cycle. Applications for renewal of enrollment must be submitted between November 1 and January 31 prior to April 1 of the year that the next enrollment cycle begins.

The last digit of a practitioner's Social Security Number determines when he must renew enrollment. If the candidate's SSN ends in:

- 0, 1, 2, or 3 – The next enrollment cycle begins April 1, 2013.
- 4, 5, or 6 – The next enrollment cycle begins April 1, 2014.

- 7, 8, or 9 – The next enrollment cycle begins April 1, 2015.

EAs who do not have an SSN must use the "7, 8, or 9" renewal schedule.

As part of the application process, the IRS will check the candidate's filing history to verify that he has filed and paid all federal taxes on time. If the practitioner owns or has an interest in a business, the IRS will also check the tax compliance history of the business. In addition, the IRS will check that the EA has completed all necessary professional continuing education requirements.

Renewal Requirements

The IRS will send a reminder notice when an EA is due for renewal. However, failing to receive a reminder notice of the renewal requirement does not excuse the EA from the obligation to re-apply. An EA is expected to inform the Return Preparer Office of address changes within 60 days of a move to make sure he receives timely reminder notices.

Preparers may lose their eligibility to practice before the IRS for the following reasons, among others:

- Failure to meet the yearly educational requirements for enrollment.
- Failure to renew a PTIN or pay required fees.
- Requesting to be placed on inactive/retirement status.
- Being disbarred by state regulatory agencies (in the case of attorneys and CPAs). An attorney or CPA who is disbarred from practice at the state level is also disbarred from practice at the federal level, and cannot practice before the IRS as long as their disbarment (or suspension) is active.

To renew, an EA must file Form 8554, *Application for Renewal of Enrollment to Practice before the Internal Revenue Service*, and submit the required nonrefundable fee. Even if an application is ultimately denied, the fee will not be refunded.

Inactive and Terminated EAs

The RPO will notify any EAs who fail to comply with the requirements for eligibility for renewal of enrollment. The notice via First Class mail will explain the reason for noncompliance and will provide the individual an opportunity to furnish the requested information, such as missing CE credits, in writing. An EA has 60 days from the date of the notice to respond to this initial warning. If no response is received, the EA will move to "inactive" status as of April 1.

To be eligible for renewal after missing one full enrollment cycle, an EA must pay a fee for both the prior and current renewal cycle and verify that the required CE hours have been taken.

Each year on April 1, the RPO will issue letters to all EAs who have missed two renewal cycles to advise them that their EA status is terminated. To have their termination status reconsidered, EAs must file a written protest within 30 days with the OPR and provide a valid reason for not enrolling timely. Reasons may include serious illness and extended travel out of the country.

Continuing Education (CE) for Enrolled Agents

During each three-year enrollment cycle, an EA must complete 72 hours of continuing education credit. A minimum of 16 hours, including two hours of ethics or professional conduct, must be completed during each enrollment year.

For new EAs, the month of initial enrollment begins the CE requirement. They must complete two hours of CE for each month enrolled, which must include two hours of ethics. Enrollment for any part of a month is considered enrollment for the entire month. When an EA's new three-year enrollment cycle begins, he will be required to satisfy the full 72-hour continuing education credit requirement.

Example: Don applied to become a new EA on September 30, 2012, which also happened to be the third year of his enrollment cycle. He is required to take two hours of CE a month prior to January 1, 2013, equaling eight hours total for the months of September, October, November, and December. Two of those hours must be on the topic of ethics. Since his initial enrollment came during the final year of his enrollment cycle, Don will be required to renew his enrollment status in 2013.

If a candidate takes more than two hours of ethics courses during a single year, the additional ethics courses will count toward the yearly requirement. However, an enrolled agent may not take additional ethics courses in the current year and neglect to take them in future years. Ethics courses must be taken *every year*.

Exception: If a practitioner *retakes and passes* the EA exam again since his last renewal, he is only required to take 16 hours of CE, including two hours of ethics, during the last year of his current enrollment cycle.

CE Coursework

In order to qualify as professional CE, a course must be designed to enhance professional knowledge in federal taxation or federal tax-related matters. Courses related to state taxation do not meet the IRS's requirement, unless at least 80% of the program material consists of a comparison between federal and state tax laws.

All individuals and companies who wish to offer continuing education to EAs must pay a registration fee and apply to be approved as providers, including accredited educational institutions. Providers approved by the IRS are issued a provider number and are allowed to display a logo that says "IRS Approved Continuing Education Provider." [23]

Qualifying programs include traditional seminars and conferences, as well as correspondence or individual self-study programs on the Internet, so long as they are approved courses of study by approved providers.

All continuing education programs are measured in terms of "contact hours." The shortest recognized program is one hour. In order for a course to qualify for CE credit, it must feature at least 50 minutes of continuous participation. A qualified course may also be longer than an hour; for example, a course lasting longer than 50 minutes but less than 80 minutes still counts as only one contact hour.

Individual segments at conferences and conventions are considered one total program. For example, two 90-minute segments (180 minutes) at a continuous conference count as three contact hours. For a university or college course, each semester hour credit equals 15 contact hours and a quarter-hour credit equals ten contact hours.

A tax professional may also receive continuing education credit for serving as an instructor, discussion leader, or speaker on federal tax matters for approved educational programs. One hour of CE credit is awarded for each contact hour

---

[23] The IRS contracts with a private company to maintain an updated list of qualified providers at https://ssl.kinsail.com/partners/irs/publicListing.asp.

completed. Two hours of CE credit is awarded for actual subject preparation time for each contact hour completed as an instructor, discussion leader, or speaker at such programs.

The maximum credit for instruction and preparation may not exceed six hours annually for EAs. Individuals claiming this credit need to maintain records to verify preparation time.

CE Participant and Provider Recordkeeping Requirements

After completing CE coursework, an EA will receive a certificate from the course provider. Any programs that an EA has taken will be reported to the IRS by the approved course provider, using the PTINs of the individual participants. Course providers must renew their status every year.

In 2012, the IRS allowed PTIN holders to self-attest that they met the yearly CE requirement. However, beginning in mid-2013, the IRS says that tax professionals will be able to check their online PTIN accounts to see a display of the 2013 CE programs they have completed and reported by providers. (Hours from 2012 and prior years will not be included.)

Individuals applying for renewal of enrollment must retain their CE records for four years following the date of renewal. Records should include the following information:

- The name of the CE provider organization
- The location of the program
- The title of the program, approval number received for the program, and copy of the program content
- Written outlines, course syllabi, etc. required for the program
- The date(s) attended
- The credit hours claimed
- The name(s) of the instructors, speakers, or discussion leaders
- The certificate of completion and/or signed statement of the hours of attendance obtained from the continuing education provider

CE providers also are required to maintain detailed records for four years after coursework is completed. These records must include the first and last name and the PTINs of each participant, as well as the hours completed by program.

CE Waiver

A waiver of CE requirements may be requested from the RPO in extraordinary circumstances. Qualifying circumstances include:

- Health issues
- Extended active military duty
- Absence from the United States for employment or other reasons
- Other reasons on a case-by-case basis

The request for a waiver must be accompanied by appropriate documentation, such as medical records or military paperwork. If the request is denied, the enrolled agent will be placed on the inactive roster. If the request is accepted, the EA will receive an updated enrollment card reflecting his renewal.

Example: Cristian is an EA who is also an Army reservist. He was called to active duty in a combat zone for two years. During this time, he was unable to complete his CE requirements for his enrolled agent license. Cristian requested a waiver based on his deployment, which was granted by the RPO. Cristian was granted renewal of his EA license based on extraordinary circumstances.

Unit 2: Questions

1. Enrolled agents must complete continuing education credits for renewed enrollment. Which of the following describes the credit requirements?

A. A minimum of 72 hours must be completed in each year of an enrollment cycle.
B. A minimum of 24 hours must be completed in each year of an enrollment cycle.
C. A minimum of 80 hours must be completed, overall, for the entire enrollment cycle.
D. A minimum of 16 hours must be completed in each year of the enrollment cycle, including two hours of ethics.

The answer is D. A minimum of 16 hours of continuing education credit, including two hours of ethics, must be completed in *each year* of the enrollment cycle. An EA must complete a minimum of 72 hours of continuing education during each three-year period. ###

2. Each EA who applies for renewal to practice before the IRS must retain information about CE hours completed. How long must CE verification be retained?

A. For one year following the enrollment renewal date.
B. For four years following the enrollment renewal date.
C. For five years if it is an initial enrollment.
D. The individual is not required to retain the information if the CE provider has agreed to retain it.

The answer is B. Each individual applying for renewal must retain information about CE hours completed for four years following the enrollment renewal date. The CE provider must also retain records for four years. ###

3. What is the "enrollment cycle" for EAs?

A. The enrollment cycle is the year after the effective date of renewal.
B. The enrollment cycle means the three successive enrollment years preceding the effective date of renewal.
C. The enrollment cycle is the method by which the RPO approves exam candidates.
D. The enrollment cycle is the method by which Prometric chooses the exam questions for EA candidates.

The answer is B. The "enrollment cycle" means the three successive enrollment years preceding the effective date of renewal. After the initial enrollment renewal period, regular renewal enrollments are required every three years. This is known as an enrollment cycle. ###

4. EAs who do not comply with the requirements for renewal of enrollment will be contacted by the Return Preparer Office. How much time does the EA have to respond to the RPO?

A. 30 days from the date of the notice.
B. 60 days from the date of the notice.
C. 60 days from the date of receipt.
D. 90 days from the date of the notice.

The answer is B. Enrolled agents who fail to comply with the requirements for eligibility for renewal of enrollment will be notified by the Return Preparer Office through First Class mail. The notice will explain the reason for non-compliance. The enrolled agent has 60 days from the date of the notice to respond. ###

5. Nathan, an EA, teaches various continuing education courses in tax law. What is the maximum CE credit for instruction and preparation that Nathan can claim each year?

A. Two hours.
B. Four hours.
C. Six hours.
D. Eight hours.

The answer is C. The maximum CE credit for instruction and preparation is limited to six hours a year for enrolled agents. ###

6. All of the following are potential grounds for denial of enrollment except:

A. Failure to timely file tax returns.
B. Failure to pay taxes.
C. Felony convictions.
D. A candidate who is only 18 years old.

The answer is D. The minimum age for enrollment is 18, so anyone over 17 would not be denied enrollment based on his age. Failure to timely file tax returns, pay taxes, or felony convictions are all potential grounds for denying an application for enrollment. The RPO will review all of the facts and circumstances to determine whether a denial of enrollment is warranted. ###

7. To maintain active enrollment to practice before the IRS, each practitioner is required to have his enrollment renewed. The Return Preparer Office will notify practitioners of their need to renew. Which of the following statements about renewal of enrollment is correct?

A. The RPO may charge a reasonable refundable fee for each application for renewal of enrollment.
B. Failure by a practitioner to receive notification from the RPO of the renewal requirement is not justification for the failure to renew enrollment in a timely manner.
C. Forms required for renewal may only be obtained from the National Association of Enrolled Agents.
D. The enrollment cycle is a three-year period, and all EAs must renew at the same time, no matter when they first became enrolled.

The answer is B. Application for renewal is required to maintain active renewal status. Not receiving notice of the renewal requirement does not excuse the EA from having to reapply. Failure to receive notification from the RPO of the renewal requirement will not be justification for the failure to renew enrollment in a timely manner. The renewal fee is nonrefundable, even if enrollment is not granted. ###

8. Chris earned his initial enrollment in year three of his enrollment cycle, in the month of November. How many CE credits must he complete before the end of the year?

A. Four CE credits, of which two must be ethics courses.
B. Six CE credits, of which two must be ethics courses.
C. Sixteen CE credits, of which two must be ethics courses.
D. Two CE credits, of which one must be ethics courses.

The answer is A. Chris is required to complete four CE credits for November and December of the third year, of which two must be ethics courses. In his next renewal cycle, Chris will be required to complete a minimum of 72 hours of continuing education credits, which encompasses three calendar years. (Note: A minimum of 16 hours of continuing education credits including two hours of ethics or professional conduct credits must be completed during each enrollment year of an enrollment cycle.) ###

9. Andrea has been enrolled to practice before the IRS for many years. Her records show that she had the following hours of qualified CE in 2012:

| January 2012, 7 hrs: General tax CE |
| May 2012, 1 hr: Ethics |
| December 2012, 9 hrs: General tax CE |

Has Andrea met her minimum yearly CE requirements?

A. Yes, Andrea has met her minimum yearly CE requirements.
B. No, Andrea has met her ethics requirement, but not the overall minimum requirement for the year.
C. No, Andrea has not met her ethics requirement.
D. None of the above.

The answer is C. The IRS enforces a 16-hour minimum per year, and requires two hours of ethics per year. Andrea has only completed one hour of ethics CE. She has met her yearly "general" CE requirement, but she has not met the ethics requirement for the year, so her minimum requirements have not been met. ###

10. A practitioner's status as an enrolled agent must be renewed every three years as determined by _____.

A. His last name.
B. The last digit of his Social Security Number.
C. The date of his initial enrollment.
D. The date that he passed the EA exam.

The answer is B. A practitioner's status as an enrolled agent must be renewed every three years as determined by the last digit of his Social Security Number. ###

11. Under Circular 230, an applicant who wishes to challenge the Return Preparer Office's denial of his application for enrollment is required to do which of the following?

A. File a written appeal with the Secretary of the Treasury.
B. File a written appeal with the Office of Professional Responsibility.
C. File a written appeal with the Commissioner of the IRS.
D. Resubmit another application within 30 days.

The answer is B. An enrolled agent who is initially denied enrollment and wishes to challenge the denial must file a written appeal with the Office of Professional Responsibility. ###

12. A minimum of how many hours of ethics education are required per enrollment cycle?

A. Seventy-two.
B. Forty-eight.
C. Eight.
D. Six.

The answer is D. In order to maintain their licenses, EAs must complete at least two hours of ethics education every year. Therefore, within a *three-year cycle*, an EA must complete at least six hours of ethics (minimum two hours per year). The IRS enforces a 16-hour CE minimum per year and requires AT LEAST two hours of ethics per year. ###

13. Jasmine applied for her initial enrollment during an enrollment cycle. How many continuing education credits must she complete?

A. Three hours of qualifying continued education credits per month, including two hours of ethics or professional conduct credits per year.
B. One hour of qualifying continued education credit per month, including two hours of ethics or professional conduct credits per year.
C. Two hours of qualifying continued education credits per month, including two hours of ethics or professional conduct credits per year.
D. Four hours of qualifying continued education credits per month, including two hours of ethics or professional conduct credits per year.

The answer is C. If initial enrollment occurs during an enrollment cycle, the EA is required to complete two hours of qualifying continued education credits per month, including two hours of ethics or professional conduct credits per year. When the new three-year enrollment cycle begins, he will be required to satisfy the regular 72-hour continuing education credit requirements. In order for an individual to maintain enrollment status, a minimum of 72 hours of continuing education credits must be completed during each enrollment cycle, which includes a minimum of two hours of ethics per year. ###

14. What action should an EA take if he chooses to appeal termination from enrollment?

A. Call the Office of Professional Responsibility to complain.
B. File a written protest within 30 days of the date of the notice of termination.
C. File a written protest within 60 days of the date of the notice of termination.
D. File a written protest within 90 days of the date of the notice of termination.

The answer is B. An EA who has been terminated from enrollment by the OPR should file a written protest within 30 days of the date of the notice. The protest must be filed with the Office of Professional Responsibility. ###

15. Eleanor failed to complete her continuing education requirements. She plans to request a waiver so that she can renew her EA license. All of the following are reasons the RPO will typically accept as it considers whether to grant her waiver except:

A. Financial hardship.
B. Absence from the United States for an extended period of time.
C. Back surgery that required lengthy rehabilitation.
D. Deployment to Afghanistan as a member of the Army Reserve.

The answer is A. Although the RPO will consider each waiver request on a case-by-case basis, it will typically grant waivers based on the following reasons: active military duty; absence from the U.S. for an extended period of time, provided the individual doesn't practice before the IRS during that absence; and health issues. Financial hardship is not generally considered a legitimate reason for someone not to complete her CE requirements. ###

16. Chung, an EA, retakes the SEE in the second year of his renewal, and achieves passing scores. How many hours of continuing education must he take during the final year of his enrollment cycle?

A. Four.
B. Eight.
C. Ten.
D. Sixteen.

The answer is D. There is an exception to the mandated 72 hours of continuing education credit required per enrollment cycle. An enrolled agent who retakes the EA exam and has passing scores on each part only has to do 16 hours of CE during the final year of his enrollment cycle, including two hours of ethics training. ###

17. When does a new EA's enrollment take effect?

A. On the date he applies for enrollment with the IRS.
B. On the date listed on his Treasury card.
C. On the date he receives his Treasury card.
D. On the first day of January after he receives his Treasury card.

The answer is B. An EA's enrollment becomes official on the date listed on his Treasury card, whether he has actually received the card or not. ###

18. Angela is taking a continuing education course that combines updates on new Kansas state law and on federal tax law. In order to satisfy the enrolled agent CE requirements, the following is true:

A. The course must be taken in person at a conference or workshop. An online self-study course is not allowed.
B. The course must be given by an approved CE provider who is a CPA.
C. The course must be given by an approved CE provider and must include at least 50% updates on federal tax law.
D. The course must be given by an approved CE provider and must include at least 80% updates on federal tax law.

The answer is D. All CE for credit must be given by an approved provider, whether in person, online, or in a self-study program. The course material must focus on federal tax law. If a course also deals with individual state law, at least 80% of the program material must consist of a comparison between federal and state tax laws. ###

19. Cameron is an EA whose Social Security Number ends with the number seven. When does the next cycle begin for him to renew his enrollment?

A. On the anniversary date of his initial enrollment.
B. Beginning April 1, 2014.
C. Beginning April 1, 2015.
D. Beginning April 1, 2016.

The answer is C. For EAs whose Social Security Numbers end in 7, the next enrollment cycle begins April 1, 2015. If the candidate's SSN ends in:

•0, 1, 2, or 3 – The next enrollment cycle begins April 1, 2013.
•4, 5, or 6 – The next enrollment cycle begins April 1, 2014.
•7, 8, or 9 – The next enrollment cycle begins April 1, 2015.

EAs who do not have an SSN must use the "7, 8, or 9" renewal schedule. ###

Unit 3: Tax Preparer Responsibilities

More Reading:

Publication 4019, *Third Party Authorization, Levels of Authority*

Publication 947, *Practice Before the IRS and Power of Attorney*

Publication 216, *Conference and Practice Requirements*

The Treasury Department's Circular 230 sets forth regulations that govern enrolled agents, CPAs, attorneys, and others who practice before the IRS. As of 2011, the rules of Circular 230 are applied to all paid tax preparers.

Circular 230 imposes professional standards and codes of conduct for tax preparers and tax advisors. It prohibits certain actions, requires other actions, and details penalties for ethical and other violations by tax preparers.

Central to the Circular 230 regulations is the mandate for practitioners to exercise **due diligence** when performing the following duties:

- Preparing or assisting in the preparing, approving, and filing of returns, documents, affidavits, and other papers relating to IRS matters.
- Determining the correctness of oral or written representations made by the client, and also for positions taken on the tax return.

Best Practices

Circular 230 explains the broad concept of "best practices." Tax advisors must provide clients with the highest quality representation concerning federal tax matters by adhering to best practices in providing advice and in preparing documents or information for the IRS.

Tax preparers who oversee a firm's practice should take reasonable steps to ensure that the firm's procedures for all employees are consistent with best practices. "Best practices" include the following:

- Communicating clearly with the client regarding the terms of the engagement.
- Establishing the facts, determining which facts are relevant, evaluating the reasonableness of any assumptions, relating the applicable law to the relevant facts, and arriving at a conclusion supported by the law and the facts.

- Advising the client of the conclusions reached and the impact of the advice rendered; for example, advising whether a taxpayer may avoid accuracy-related penalties if he relies on the advice provided.
- Acting fairly and with integrity in practice before the IRS.

The Duty to Advise (§10.21 Knowledge of client's omission)

A practitioner who knows that his client has not complied with the revenue laws or who has made an error or omission on his tax return has the responsibility to advise the client promptly of the noncompliance, error, or omission, as well as the *consequences* of the error.

Under the rules of Circular 230 §10.21, the tax practitioner is not responsible for fixing the noncompliance once he has notified the client of the issue. The tax professional is also not responsible for notifying the IRS of noncompliance by a client.

Example: Jeremy is an EA with a new client, Monique, who has self-prepared her own returns in the past. Jeremy notices that Monique has been claiming head of household on her tax returns, but she does not qualify for this status, because she does not have a qualifying person. Jeremy is required to promptly notify Monique of the error and tell her the consequences of not correcting the error. However, Jeremy is not required to amend Monique's prior year tax returns to correct the error. Nor is he required to notify the IRS of Monique's claim of incorrect status.

The §10.21 obligations are not limited to practitioners preparing returns, so the discovery of an error or omission in the course of a tax consulting or advisory engagement will also trigger its requirements.

Example: Gina is an EA who takes over another tax preparer's practice. She discovers that the previous preparer has been taking Section 179 depreciation on assets that do not qualify for this bonus depreciation treatment. Gina must notify her clients of the error and the consequences of not correcting the error. She is not required to correct the error.

A tax professional may rely on the work product of another tax preparer. A practitioner will be presumed to have exercised due diligence if he uses reasonable care in revaluating the work product of the other practitioner.

Other Duties and Prohibited Acts

Performance as a notary §10.26: A tax practitioner who is a notary public and is employed as counsel, attorney, or agent in a matter before the IRS or who has a material interest in the matter cannot engage in any notary activities related to that matter.

Negotiations of taxpayer refund checks §10.31: Tax return preparers must not endorse or negotiate (cash) any refund check issued to the taxpayer. A preparer faces a $500 fine for each time he improperly cashes a taxpayer's check.

No delay tactics allowed: A practitioner must not delay the prompt disposition of any matter before the IRS.

No employment of disbarred persons: A tax practitioner may not knowingly employ a person or accept assistance from a person who has been disbarred or suspended from practice. This restriction applies even if the duties of the disbarred or suspended person would not include actual preparation of tax returns.

Practice of law §10.32: Nothing in the regulations or in Circular 230 may be construed as authorizing persons not attorneys to practice law.

Confidentiality Privilege for Enrolled Practitioners

Enrolled practitioners and their clients are granted confidentiality protection. This confidentiality privilege applies to attorneys, CPAs, enrolled agents, enrolled actuaries, and certain other individuals allowed to practice before the IRS.[24]

The confidentiality protection applies to communications that would be considered privileged if they were between the taxpayer and an attorney and that relate to:

- Noncriminal tax matters before the IRS, or
- Noncriminal tax proceedings brought in federal court by or against the United States.

---

[24]IRC Section 7525.

The confidentiality privilege does not apply:

- In criminal tax matters
- To any written communications regarding the promotion of a tax shelter
- To the general preparation of tax returns
- In state tax proceedings

This confidentiality privilege cannot be used with any agency other than the IRS.

Conflicts of Interest §10.29

A tax professional may represent conflicting interests before the IRS only if all the parties offer their consent in writing. If there is any potential conflict of interest, the practitioner must disclose the existence of a financial interest and be given the opportunity to disclose all material facts.

A conflict of interest exists if:

- The representation of one client will be adverse to another client; or
- There is a significant risk that the representation of one or more clients will be materially limited by the practitioner's responsibilities to another client, a former client, or another third person.
- The representation of the taxpayer would be in conflict with the tax preparer's personal interests.

The consent must be obtained in writing and retained for at least 36 months from the date representation ends. At minimum, the consent should adequately describe the nature of the conflict and the parties the practitioner represents. The practitioner may still represent a client when a conflict of interest exists if:

- The practitioner reasonably believes that he will be able to provide competent and diligent representation to each affected client;
- The representation is not prohibited by law; and
- Each affected client waives the conflict of interest and gives informed consent, confirmed in writing.

> **Example:** Christa is an EA who prepares tax returns for Jana and Brett, a married couple. In 2012, they go through a contentious divorce, and Christa believes there is a potential for conflict of interest relating to the tax advice she would give them. She prepares a written statement explaining the potential conflict of interest. Jana and Bret still want Christa to prepare their returns, so she has her clients sign the written consent. Christa must retain the record of their consent for at least 36 months.

Strict Privacy of Taxpayer Information: Section 7216

The IRS has enacted strict privacy regulations designed to give taxpayers more control over their personal information and tax records. The regulations limit tax professionals' use and disclosure of client information, and explain precise and limited exceptions in which disclosure is permitted.

Internal Revenue Code §7216 is a **criminal provision** enacted by Congress that prohibits tax return preparers from knowingly or recklessly disclosing or using tax return information. The regulations were updated in 2008 to clarify that e-file providers are among the return preparers who are bound by these privacy rules.

A convicted preparer may be fined up to $1,000, imprisoned up to one year, or both, for *each violation* of Section 7216. There is also a civil penalty of $250 for improper disclosure or use of taxpayer information, outlined in IRC §6713. However, this code does not require that the disclosure be "knowing or reckless" as it does under Section 7216.

Tax preparers must generally obtain written consent from taxpayers before they can disclose information to a third party or use the information for anything other than the actual preparation of tax returns. The actual consent form must meet the following guidelines:

- Identify the purpose of the disclosure.
- Identify the recipient and describe the authorized information.
- Include the name of the preparer and the name of the taxpayer.
- Include mandatory language that informs the taxpayer that he is not required to sign the consent, and if he does sign the consent, he can set a time period for the duration of that consent.

- Include mandatory language that refers the taxpayer to the Treasury Inspector General for Tax Administration if he believes that his tax return information has been disclosed or used improperly.
- If applicable, inform the taxpayer that his tax return information may be disclosed to a tax return preparer located outside the U.S.
- Be signed and dated by the taxpayer. Electronic (online) consents must be in the same type as the website's standard text and contain the taxpayer's affirmative consent (as opposed to an "opt-out" clause).

Unless a specific time period is specified, consent is valid for one year.

These updated privacy regulations apply to paid preparers, electronic return originators, tax software developers, and other persons or entities engaged in tax preparation. The regulations also apply to most volunteer tax preparers, for example, Volunteer Income Tax Assistance and Tax Counseling for the Elderly volunteers, and employees and contractors employed by tax preparation companies in a support role.

Allowable Disclosures

In certain circumstances, a preparer may disclose information to a second taxpayer who appears on a tax return. The preparer may disclose return information obtained from the first taxpayer if:

- The second taxpayer is related to the first taxpayer.
- The first taxpayer's interest is not adverse to the second taxpayer's interest.
- The first taxpayer has not prohibited the disclosure.

> **Example:** Zach is an EA with two married clients, Serena and Tyler, who file jointly. Serena works long hours, so she is unavailable when Tyler meets with Zach to prepare their joint tax return. Later, Serena comes in alone to sign the return. She also has a quick question regarding the mortgage interest on a tax return. Zach is allowed to disclose return information to Serena because the tax return is a joint return, both of their names are on the return, and Tyler has not prohibited any disclosures.

A taxpayer is considered "related" to another taxpayer in any of the following relationships:

- Husband and wife, or child and parent
- Grandchild and grandparent
- General partner in a partnership
- Trust or estate and the beneficiary
- A corporation and shareholder
- Members of a controlled group of corporations

A tax preparer may also disclose tax return information that was obtained from a first taxpayer in preparing a tax return of the second taxpayer, if the preparer has obtained written consent from the first taxpayer. For example, if an unmarried couple lives together and splits the mortgage interest, the preparer may use or disclose information from the first taxpayer to the second so long as the preparer has written consent.

The Definition of "Tax Return Information"

The IRS's definition of "tax return information" is broad and encompasses the following:

"All the information tax return preparers obtain from taxpayers or other sources in any form or matter that is used to prepare tax returns or is obtained in connection with the preparation of returns. It also includes all computations, worksheets, and printouts preparers create; correspondence from the IRS during the preparation, filing and correction of returns; statistical compilations of tax return information; and tax return preparation software registration information."

All of this tax return information is protected by §7216 and its regulations.

When Disclosure Permissions Are Not Required

A tax preparer is not required to obtain disclosure permission from a client if the disclosure is made for any of the following reasons:

- A court order or subpoena issued by any court of record whether at the federal, state, or local level. The required information must be clearly identified in the document (subpoena or court order) in order for a preparer to disclose information.

73

- An administrative order, demand, summons, or subpoena that is issued by any federal agency, state agency, or commission charged under the laws of the state with licensing, registration, or regulation of tax return preparers.
- In order to report a crime to proper authorities. Even if the preparer is mistaken and no crime exists, if the preparer makes the disclosure in good faith, he will not be subject to sanctions.
- Confidential information for the purpose of peer reviews.

A tax preparer may disclose private client information to his attorney or to an employee of the IRS, subsequent to an investigation of the tax return preparer conducted by the IRS.

Example: The IRS is investigating a CPA named Harry for possible misconduct. Harry has an attorney who is assisting in his defense. In reality, Harry was the victim of embezzlement because his bookkeeper was stealing client checks. Harry discovered the embezzlement when the IRS contacted him about client complaints. Harry may disclose confidential client information to his attorney in order to assist with his own defense. Harry may also disclose confidential client information to the IRS during the course of its investigation.

A tax preparer may disclose tax return information to a tax return processor. For example, if a tax preparer uses an electronic or tax return processing service, he may disclose tax return information to that service in order to prepare tax returns or compute tax liability.

A tax preparer may also solicit additional business from a taxpayer in matters not related to the IRS (for example, if the preparer offers other financial services such as bookkeeping or insurance services). However, the tax preparer must obtain written consent from the taxpayer in order to make these solicitations.

Example: Juliet is an EA who also sells life insurance. She obtains a written consent from her client, Manuel, and then sends him a solicitation by mail for her insurance services. This is allowed because Juliet obtained written consent from Manuel in advance.

Third Party Authorizations

A "third party authorization" is when a taxpayer authorizes an individual (usually his tax preparer) to communicate with the IRS on his behalf. A third party authorization is different from a regular power of attorney in a number of ways. Third party authorizations include but are not limited to:

- The Third Party Designee (sometimes referred to as "Check Box" authority)
- The Oral Disclosure Consent (ODC)
- The Oral Tax Information Authorization (OTIA)[25]

The third party designee authorization allows the IRS to discuss the processing of a taxpayer's current tax return, including the status of refunds, with whomever the taxpayer specifies. The authorization automatically expires on the due date of the next tax return.

A taxpayer can choose a third party designee by checking the "yes" box on his tax return, which is why it is known as "Check Box" authority. The taxpayer then enters the designee's name and phone number and a self-selected five-digit PIN, which the designee must confirm when requesting information from the IRS.

Currently, the third party designee authorization is not recorded on the CAF system. Instead, during tax return processing, the authorization is recorded directly onto the taxpayer's account.

The designee can exchange verbal information with the IRS on return processing issues and on refunds and payments related to the return. The designee may also receive written account information, including transcripts upon request.

---

[25] IRC 6103(e)(6) and (c) provide for disclosures to powers of attorney and other designees.

Example: Rashid named his EA, Patty, as his third party designee on his tax return. A few months after filing his return, Rashid still had not received his refund. He asked Patty if she could check the status of his refund. Patty called the IRS and was given the information over the phone, because she was listed as a third party designee on Rashid's return. No further authorization was necessary for Patty to receive this confidential taxpayer information.

The third party designee authorization can co-exist with a power of attorney for the same tax and tax period. However, the authorization does not allow the designee to "represent the taxpayer." Although it is similar to the authority given by Form 8821, *Tax Information Authorization* (TIA), it is more limited. Unlike the third party designee authorization, Form 8821 can be used to allow discussions with third parties and disclosures of information to third parties on matters other than just a taxpayer's current return.

Note: There is a significant difference between a third party designee and an "official representative." A power of attorney (Form 2848) allows a practitioner to represent and negotiate with the IRS on the taxpayer's behalf. An authorized representative (listed on Form 2848) may advocate for the taxpayer and may argue facts or law with the IRS. The appointee of a Tax Information Authorization (Form 8821 or third party designee) is only able to receive and exchange information with the IRS for purposes of resolving basic tax account issues.[26]

A taxpayer may give oral consent for the IRS to speak with a third party if necessary to resolve a federal tax matter.[27] However, oral consent does not substitute for a power of attorney or a legal designation, and the discussion is limited to the issue for which the consent is given.

The Oral Tax Information Authorization (OTIA) is the "verbal equivalent" of Form 8821 and is valid until revoked or withdrawn. The OTIA allows the taxpayer the ability to grant a third party, including friends and family, the authority to receive and inspect both written and verbal tax account information. The appointee must have a CAF number. The appointee may receive copies of notices and tran-

---

[26] See Publication 4019 for a handy quick reference of third party authorizations.

[27] Public Law 104-168, commonly known as the Taxpayer Bill of Rights II, deleted the requirement that a taxpayer's request for disclosure to a third party be in writing. The change was not possible until Temporary Regulation 301-6103(c)-IT, effective January 11, 2001, which authorized the IRS to accept non-written requests or consents, authorizing the disclosure of return information to third parties assisting taxpayers to resolve federal tax related matters. The temporary regulation was made permanent by 26 CFR 301.6103(c) 1 (c).

scripts on open issues, but cannot receive IRS refund checks. The OTIA is recorded on the CAF.

The Oral Disclosure Consent (ODC) is a tax information authorization limited to specific notices and oral disclosure only. The ODC does not allow the appointee to receive any written information and does not allow the appointee to represent the taxpayer. It is not recorded on the CAF. It is recorded directly on the account.

When only requesting the disclosure of return information such as copies of tax returns, transcripts of an account to verify adjusted gross income, and wages earned for *nontax matter purposes* (such as income verification and loan applications), the taxpayer should use Form 4506, *Request for a Copy or Transcript of Tax Form*, and submit it to the IRS Return and Income Verification Services.

Summary: Types of Consents

1. **Third Party Designee Authorization** is submitted with the filing of a tax return for the purpose of resolving return processing, payment, or refund issues.

2. **Oral Disclosure Consent** is used when addressing a specific issue raised in a notice received from the IRS. This type of consent is usually done with the taxpayer over the phone.

3. **Oral Tax Information Authorization or Form 8821** is used when an examination of written account information is needed and the issues are related to the tax period versus a specific notice issue. In actual practice, this form is used most often to obtain taxpayer records or transcripts of prior returns.

4. **Power of Attorney (Form 2848)** is used when the authorization is for the purpose of allowing a tax professional (attorney, CPA, EA, etc.) to represent and act on behalf of the taxpayer, including negotiating with the IRS, signing returns, consents, and arguing facts or law. This is the most formal of all the consents. If properly authorized, Form 2848 allows enrolled practitioners unlimited practice rights to represent taxpayers.

IRS Information Requests § 10.20

Under Circular 230 §10.20, when the IRS requests information, a practitioner must comply and submit records promptly.

If the requested information or records are not in the practitioner's possession, he must promptly advise the requesting IRS officer and provide any information he has regarding the identity of the person who may have possession or control of the requested information or records. The practitioner must also make a "reasonable inquiry" of his client regarding the location of the requested records.

However, the practitioner is not required to make inquiry of any other person or to independently verify any information furnished by his client. The practitioner is also not required to contact any third party who might be in possession of the records.

> **Example:** An IRS revenue agent recently submitted a lawful records request to Randall, an EA, for accounting records relating to a former client that was under IRS investigation. However, Randall had fired his former client for nonpayment and then returned his client's records. Randall promptly notified the IRS officer that he no longer had possession of the records. Randall also attempted to contact his former client, but the phone number was disconnected. Randall is not required to contact any third parties to discover the location of the requested records. Therefore, Randall has fulfilled his obligations under §10.20.

A practitioner may not interfere with any lawful effort by the IRS to obtain any record or information *unless* the practitioner believes in good faith and on reasonable grounds that the record or information is privileged under IRC Section 7525. A practitioner can also be exempted from these rules if he believes in good faith that the request is of doubtful legality.

If the OPR requests information concerning possible violations of the regulations by other parties, such as other preparers or taxpayers, the practitioner must furnish the information and be prepared to testify in disbarment or suspension proceedings.

Return of Client Records (§10.28)

A tax practitioner is *required* to return a client's records whether or not fees have been paid. Client records are defined as any original records belonging to the client, including any work product that the client has already *paid for*, such as a completed copy of a tax return.

The practitioner must, at the request of a client, promptly return any and all records that are necessary for the client to comply with his federal tax obligations. The practitioner must also allow the client reasonable access to review and copy any additional records retained by the practitioner that are necessary for the client to comply with his federal tax obligations.

The practitioner may retain copies of the records returned to a client.

A fee dispute does not relieve the practitioner of his responsibility to return client records. The practitioner must provide the client with reasonable access to review and copy any additional records retained by the practitioner under state law that are necessary for the client to comply with his federal tax obligations.

Client records do not include the tax practitioner's work product. "Records of the client" include:

- All documents provided to the practitioner that pre-existed the retention of the practitioner by the client.
- Any materials that were prepared by the client or a third party at any time and provided to the practitioner relating to the subject matter of the representation.
- Any document prepared by the practitioner that was presented to the client relating to a prior representation if such document is necessary for the taxpayer to comply with his current federal tax obligations.

The term "records of the client" does not include any return, claim for refund, schedule, affidavit, appraisal, or any other document prepared by the practitioner if he is withholding these documents pending the client's payment of fees.

Example: Leroy, an EA, has a client, Samantha, who becomes very upset after he tells her she owes substantial penalties to the IRS in the current year. Samantha wants to get a second opinion, and she does not want to pay Leroy for his time. Leroy is required to hand over Samantha's tax records, including copies of her W-2 forms and any other information she brought to his office. Leroy returns her original records, but he does not give her a copy of the tax return he prepared, since she did not pay for the return. A practitioner is not required to give a client any tax return, claim for refund, schedule, affidavit, appraisal, or any other document prepared by the practitioner if he is withholding the documents because of a fee dispute.

> **Example:** Clara is an EA who does substantial tax work for a partnership, Greenway Landscaping. Greenway has been slow to pay in the past, so Clara asks that the owners of Greenway pay for the tax returns when they pick them up. Greenway refuses and demands the tax returns anyway. Clara decides to discontinue all contact with Greenway. Clara must return Greenway's original records, but she is not required to give Greenway work product that the owners have not paid for.

Retaining Copies of Tax Returns

Tax preparers are required to keep a copy (or a list) of all returns they have prepared for at least three years. Alternatively, preparers may also keep copies of the actual returns. If the preparer does not keep copies of the actual returns, he is required to keep a list or card file of clients and tax returns prepared. At a minimum, the list must contain the taxpayer's name, identification number, tax year, and the type of return prepared.

> ***Note:*** In actual practice, most preparers keep scanned, digital, or hard copies of client tax returns rather than simply a list of the returns prepared.

Signature Requirements for Preparers

A tax return preparer is required by law to furnish a completed copy of a return or claim to the taxpayer, no later than the time the return or claim is presented for the taxpayer's signature.

A paid preparer is required by law to sign the tax return and fill out the preparer areas of the form. The preparer must also include his PTIN on the return. Although the preparer signs the return, the taxpayer is ultimately responsible for the accuracy of every item on the return.

The preparer must sign the return *after* it is completed and *before* it is presented to the taxpayer for signature. If the original preparer is unavailable for signature, another preparer must review the entire preparation of the return or claim and then must manually sign it.

For the purposes of the signature requirement, the preparer with primary responsibility for the overall accuracy of the return or claim is considered the preparer, if more than one preparer is involved. The other preparers do not have to be disclosed on the return.

If a return is mechanically completed by a computer that is not under the control of the individual preparer, a manually signed attestation may be attached to the return. The signature requirement may be satisfied by a photocopy of the manually signed copy of the return or claim. The preparer must retain the signed copy. A valid signature is defined by state law and may be anything that clearly indicates the intent to sign.

A preparer may sign *on behalf of the taxpayer* in the client's signature area if certain standards are met. For example, a representative is permitted to sign a taxpayer's return if the taxpayer is unable to sign the return because of disease or injury, or continuous absence from the United States, including when a taxpayer is serving in a combat zone. When a return is signed by a representative, it must be mailed and accompanied by a power of attorney (Form 2848). A taxpayer may also assign another agent (such as a spouse or a family member) to sign his tax return, by completing a valid power of attorney.

Paid tax preparers are also required to sign payroll tax returns.

The preparer's declaration on signing the return states that the information contained in the return is true, correct, and complete based on all information the preparer has. This statement is signed under penalty of perjury.

The signature requirements for e-filed returns are covered later.

Preparer Identification (PTIN Requirement)

Paid preparers must include their PTIN with every return filed with the IRS. Previously, paid preparers had the option of using their Social Security Number. With new regulations in force, all paid preparers are now required to have a PTIN in order to prepare tax returns for a fee.

Penalties Related to Tax Return Preparation

Under IRC §6695, the IRS lists the penalties that may be assessed when it comes to the preparation of tax returns for other persons. The penalty is $50 for each violation of the following:

- Failure to furnish a copy of a return or claim to a taxpayer
- Failure to sign a return or claim for refund
- Failure to furnish an identifying number (PTIN) on a return
- Failure to retain a copy or list of a return or claim

- Failure to file correct information returns

The penalty is steeper for a preparer who endorses, cashes, or deposits a taxpayer's refund check. A preparer may be assessed a fee of $500 for each check violation. The penalty is also $500 for each failure to comply with Earned Income Credit due diligence requirements (covered in detail later in Unit 5.)

The maximum penalty imposed by the IRS on any tax return preparer cannot exceed $25,000 in a calendar year or return period.

> **Note:** Specific penalties that may be imposed on both preparers and taxpayers are often tested on the EA exam. Test-takers should be familiar with each of these penalties listed, as well as others detailed in this study guide.

Identity Theft and Preparer Security

Identity theft occurs when someone uses another individual's personally identifiable information, such as his name, Social Security Number, or credit card number, without his permission in order to commit fraud or other crimes. Fraudulent refunds have become a major issue, with the acting IRS commissioner calling identity theft one of the "biggest challenges" facing the IRS today.

In February 2013, the IRS announced the results of a year-long enforcement crackdown targeting refund fraud caused by identity theft. Hundreds of suspects were arrested in a sweep of identity theft suspects. The IRS says aggressive enforcement stopped $20 billion in fraudulent returns from being issued in 2012.

One common source of fraud is when identity thieves file fraudulent refund claims using another person's identifying information, which they have stolen. To stop identity thieves, the IRS says it now has dozens of identity theft screening filers in place to protect tax refunds. To educate taxpayers, the IRS has added a guide to identity theft on its website.

As part of its crackdown, the IRS is issuing an Identity Protection Personal Identification Number (IP PIN) to any taxpayers who have:

- reported to the IRS they have been the victims of identity theft
- given the IRS information that verifies their identity
- had an identity theft indicator applied to their account

The IP PIN helps prevent the misuse of a taxpayer's Social Security Number or Taxpayer Identification Number on tax returns. It is used on both paper and electronic returns. If a taxpayer attempts to file an electronic return without his IP PIN, the return will be rejected. If it is missing on a paper return, there is likely to be a delay in processing as the IRS will have to validate the taxpayer's identity.

The IP PIN is only valid for a single year. A taxpayer will receive a new IP PIN every year for three years after the identity theft incident. If a spouse also has an IP PIN, only the person whose SSN appears first on the tax return needs to input his or her IP PIN.

Since practitioners are required to obtain and store client information, they have an important role to play in keeping this information secure. To help prevent identity theft, preparers should confirm identities and Taxpayer Identification numbers (TINs) of taxpayers, their spouses, dependents, and EIC qualifying children contained on the returns to be prepared. TINs include Social Security Numbers (SSNs), Adopted Taxpayer Identification Numbers (ATINs), and Individual Taxpayer Identification Numbers (ITINs).

To confirm identities, the preparer can request a picture ID showing the taxpayer's name and address, and Social Security cards or other documents providing the TINs of all individuals to be listed on the return.

Additional steps practitioners can take to guard against identity theft include the following:[28]

- File clients' returns early when possible.
- E-file returns to be notified of duplicate return notices more quickly.
- Consider truncating or masking SSNs on Forms 1098, 1099, and 5498.
- Let clients know that refunds may take longer in future years as additional system security steps are taken.
- Be very careful about confirming the identity of new online clients.

Practitioner Fees

The IRS prohibits practitioners from charging "unconscionable fees." Though that term has not been defined, it is generally believed to be when the fees are so grossly unethical that the courts would consider them as such.

---

[28] *Journal of Accountancy,* February 2013.

Strict Rules for Contingent Fees

A practitioner may not charge a contingent fee (percentage of the refund) for preparing an original tax return, amended tax return, or claim for refund or credit. A contingent fee also includes a fee that is based on a percentage of the taxes saved or one that depends on a specific result.

Additionally, a contingent fee includes any fee arrangement in which the practitioner agrees to reimburse the client for all or a portion of the client's fee in the event that a position taken on a tax return or other filing is not successful. The OPR says it will aggressively seek out and sanction tax preparers who are collecting unauthorized contingent fees.

The IRS does allow a practitioner to charge a contingent fee in some limited circumstances, including:

- Representation during the examination of an original tax return; an amended return or claim for refund or credit where the amended return or claim for refund or credit was filed *within 120 days* of the taxpayer receiving a written notice of examination; or a written challenge to the original tax return.
- Services rendered in connection with a refund claim or credit or refund filed in conjunction with a penalty or interest charge.
- Services rendered in connection with any litigation or judicial proceeding arising under the Internal Revenue Code.

Advertising Restrictions §10.30

Circular 230 covers preparer advertising standards. A practitioner may not use any form of communication to advertise material that contains false, deceptive, or coercive information. Under no circumstances may practitioners use official IRS insignia in their advertising.

Enrolled agents, in describing their professional designation, may not use the term "certified" or imply any type of employment relationship with the IRS. Examples of acceptable descriptions for EAs are "enrolled to represent taxpayers before the Internal Revenue Service," "enrolled to practice before the Internal Revenue Service," and "admitted to practice before the Internal Revenue Service."

Preparers are **prohibited** from using the following logos in any capacity:

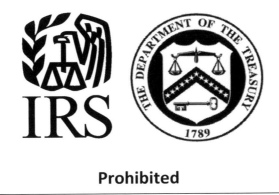

Prohibited

A practitioner may not make, directly or indirectly, an uninvited written or oral solicitation of employment in matters related to the IRS if the solicitation violates federal or state law. Practitioners have the right to make solicitations involving IRS matters in certain cases. All of the following types of communications are allowed:

- Seeking new business from a former client
- Communicating with a family member
- Targeted mailings
- Non-coercive in-person solicitation while acting as an employee, member, or officer of a 501(c)(3) or 501(c)(4) organization (such as a door-to-door fundraiser for the SPCA or a church fundraiser)

Mail solicitations are allowed, so long as the solicitation is not uninvited. In the case of direct mail and e-commerce communications, the practitioner must retain a copy of the actual communication, along with a list of persons to whom the communication was mailed or distributed, for at least 36 months.

A practitioner may attempt to solicit new business from current or former clients, or a client's family. A practitioner may not continue to contact a prospective client who has communicated he does not wish to be solicited.

Practitioners may also send solicitations to other practitioners indicating the practitioner's availability to provide professional services (such as independent contractor bookkeeping or tax preparation services). The advertising and communications must not be misleading, deceptive, or in violation of IRS regulations.

Published Fee Schedules §10.30

A practitioner may publish and advertise a fee schedule. A practitioner must adhere to the published fee schedule for *at least* 30 calendar days after it is published.

> **Example:** Gracie is an EA who publishes an advertisement in her local newspaper. The ad includes a published fee schedule for preparing certain tax return forms at a deeply discounted rate. Gracie is inundated with calls and decides that the ad was a mistake. Regardless, she must adhere to the published fee schedule for at least 30 days after it was published.

Fee information may be published in newspapers, telephone directories, mailings, websites, e-mail, or by any other method. A practitioner may include fees based on the following:

- Fixed fees for specific routine services
- Hourly fee rates
- A range of fees for particular services
- A fee charged for an initial consultation

In advertising fees on radio or television, the broadcast must be recorded, and the practitioner must retain a record of the recording for at least 36 months (three years) from the date of the last transmission or use.

> **Example:** Travis is an EA who pays for a radio commercial about his services. It plays for four months during tax season. Travis is required to keep a copy of the radio commercial for at least 36 months from the last date that the commercial aired.

Unit 3: Questions

1. If an EA knows that a client has filed an erroneous tax return, the practitioner is legally required to _____.

A. Correct the error.
B. Advise the client about the error and the consequences for not correcting the error.
C. Do nothing if the practitioner was not the one who prepared the erroneous return.
D. Disengage from any further business with the client if the client does not agree to correct the error.

The answer is B. If an EA knows that a client has filed an erroneous tax return, he must advise the client to correct the error. The EA is not required to amend the return, but he must advise the client about the error and the consequences for not correcting the error. He is not required to notify the IRS about his client's error. ###

2. Dennis, an enrolled agent, wants to hire his friend, Brandon, who is also an enrolled agent. Brandon has just been disbarred from practice by the IRS for misconduct. Brandon correctly appeals the disbarment, and his disbarment is currently under review. Which of the following statement is true?

A. Dennis can still hire Brandon as a tax preparer, so long as Brandon does not represent any taxpayers.
B. Dennis can still hire Brandon, so long as he does not sign the tax returns.
C. Dennis cannot hire Brandon.
D. Dennis can hire Brandon while he legally appeals his disbarment.

The answer is C. Dennis cannot knowingly hire a disbarred practitioner, regardless of whether that person would be preparing tax returns or not. A practitioner may not knowingly employ a person or accept employment from a person who has been disbarred or suspended by the Office of Professional Responsibility, even if that person's case is under appeal. ###

3. Which of the following statements is correct regarding a client's request for his original records in order to comply with federal tax obligations?

A. The practitioner may choose not to return records to the client even if he requests their prompt return.
B. A fee dispute relieves the practitioner of his responsibility to return a client's records.
C. The practitioner must, at the request of the client, promptly return a client's records, regardless of any fee dispute.
D. The practitioner must, at the request of the client, return client records within three months of the request.

The answer is C. Records must be returned promptly upon client demand, regardless of any fee dispute. Records are defined as any original records belonging to the client, including any work product that he has already paid for, such as a completed copy of a tax return. However, unlike in the case of the client's original documents, the practitioner is allowed to withhold the return of his own work papers or preparer work product until the client has resolved any outstanding payment issues. ###

4. Circular 230 covers which of the following topics?

A. Taxpayer identification and security.
B. Individual taxation.
C. Corporate taxation.
D. Ethics and rules of practice for tax practitioners.

The answer is D. Circular 230 covers ethics and rules of practice for tax practitioners who are enrolled to practice before the IRS. ###

5. Which of the following statements is true regarding tax practitioners?

A. EAs cannot notarize documents of the clients they represent before the IRS.
B. EAs cannot be notaries.
C. Tax preparers cannot be notaries.
D. A notary who is also a tax practitioner will not be eligible for the e-file program.

The answer is A. Tax practitioners cannot notarize documents of the clients they represent before the IRS. However, they are not prohibited from performing notary services for clients in other matters. ###

6. Which of the following statements is correct?

A. Conflicts of interest do not apply to tax professionals, only to attorneys.
B. Tax practitioners may represent clients who have a conflict of interest if waivers are signed by both parties.
C. Tax practitioners may represent clients who have a conflict of interest if the taxpayer informs both parties by phone.
D. Tax practitioners may not represent clients who have a conflict of interest.

The answer is B. A tax practitioner can represent conflict of interest clients if the clients are notified and written waivers are signed by both parties. The notification must be in writing. A phone call is insufficient. ###

7. Enrolled agents may advertise their services in the following manner:

A. With the phrase "Certified by the IRS."
B. With the phrase "Enrolled to practice before the IRS."
C. With the phrase "An IRS-approved practitioner."
D. With the phrase "A Certified Tax Accountant."

The answer is B. An EA may state that he or she is "enrolled to practice" before the Internal Revenue Service. The other phrases are not allowed. ###

8. Franklin is an EA who decides to advertise his fee schedule in the local newspaper. Which of the following fee arrangements is prohibited?

A. Hourly fee rates.
B. Fixed fees for tax preparation.
C. Contingent fee for an original return.
D. A flat fee for an initial consultation.

The answer is C. A practitioner may never charge a contingent fee for an original return that is based on the refund amount. A practitioner may publish and advertise a fee schedule. All the other fees are acceptable. ###

9. Which does not constitute a "best practice" for tax return preparers under the guidelines of Circular 230?

A. Consulting other professionals when questions arise about a particular tax issue.
B. Acting fairly and with integrity in practice before the IRS.
C. Communicating clearly with the client regarding the rules of engagement.
D. Advising the client regarding the consequences of advice rendered.

The answer is A. Although it may be a good idea to consult with other tax professionals when particular tax questions arise, this is not listed as one of the "best practices" in Circular 230. Each of the other statements is called a "best practice" in the Circular 230 regulations.

10. All of the following statements regarding the signature requirements for tax returns are correct except:

A. A tax preparer may sign a taxpayer's return in lieu of the taxpayer, if the taxpayer cannot sign his own tax return due to a physical disability.
B. A tax preparer may sign a taxpayer's return in lieu of the taxpayer, if the taxpayer cannot sign his own tax return due to an extended absence from the United States.
C. A tax preparer is allowed to copy a taxpayer's signature if he has a signed power of attorney.
D. A tax preparer must have a signed power of attorney in order to sign on the taxpayer's behalf.

The answer is C. A preparer is never allowed to copy a taxpayer's signature. This is considered forgery. A preparer may sign in lieu of the taxpayer in certain situations. For example, rules permit a representative to sign a taxpayer's return if he is unable to do so himself for any of the following reasons:
• Disease or injury
• Continuous absence from the United States (including Puerto Rico) for a period of at least 60 days prior to the date required by law for filing the return
• Other good cause if specific permission is requested of and granted by the IRS
When a return is signed by a representative, it must be accompanied by a power of attorney authorizing the representative to sign the return. ###

11. When does the authorization for a "third party designee" expire?

A. Three months after the return is filed.
B. One year after the return is filed.
C. Three years after the return is filed.
D. On the due date of the next tax return.

The answer is D. A third party designee authorization expires on the due date of the next tax return. The designee may address any issue arising out of the tax return for a period not to exceed one year from the due date of the tax return. The designee may also receive written account information including transcripts upon request. ###

12. Ryan is an EA with a client named Hannah who has had significant income from a partnership for the past five years. However, Ryan did not see a Schedule K-1 from the partnership among the information Hannah provided to him this year. What does due diligence require Ryan to do?

A. Attempt to estimate the amount that would be reported as income on the Schedule K-1 based on last year's Schedule K-1 and include that amount on Hannah's return.
B. Call Hannah's financial advisor and ask him about Hannah's investments.
C. Nothing, because Ryan is required to rely only on the information provided by his client, even if he has reason to know the information is not accurate.
D. Ask Hannah about the fact that she did not provide him with the partnership's Schedule K-1, as she had in previous years.

The answer is D. A practitioner has a "duty to advise." This means that a practitioner who knows his client has not complied with the revenue laws or has made an error in or omission from any return, document, affidavit, or other required paper has the responsibility to advise the client promptly of the noncompliance, error, or omission. ###

13. Where is the third party designee authorization recorded?

A. On the CAF system.
B. Directly onto the taxpayer's account.
C. This authorization is not recorded by the IRS; it is recorded by the practitioner.
D. The taxpayer must record the third party designee in his own account.

The answer is B. During returns processing, the authorization is recorded directly onto the account of the taxpayer. Currently, the third party designee authorization is not recorded on the CAF system. ###

14. Darrell is an EA who has a third party designee authorization for his client, Annalise. All of the following actions are allowed with this type of authorization except:

A. Darrell can receive written account information on Annalise's behalf.
B. Darrell can receive Annalise's tax transcripts upon request.
C. Darrell can check the status of tax refund processing.
D. Darrell may receive Annalise's refund check.

The answer is D. In order to receive a tax refund check on a client's behalf, a Form 2848 must be filed. A third party designee authorization is not sufficient. With a third party designee authorization, Darrell can exchange verbal information with the IRS on return processing issues and on refunds and payments related to the return. Darrell can also receive written account information, including transcripts, upon request. ###

15. Under IRC §6695, the IRS lists the penalties that may be assessed relating to the preparation of tax returns for other persons. For these violations, what is the maximum penalty per year a preparer may face?

A. $10,000.
B. $25,000.
C. $50,000.
D. $100,000.

The answer is B. Under the terms of IRC §6695, the maximum penalty imposed on any tax return preparer cannot exceed $25,000 in a calendar year for these specific violations. ###

16. What penalty does a tax return preparer face if he improperly cashes a client's tax refund check?

A. Nothing. This is acceptable so long as the client has given permission to do so.
B. A fine of $50 for each violation.
C. A fine of $100 for each violation.
D. A fine of $500 for each violation.

The answer is D. It is prohibited for return preparers to negotiate (cash) taxpayers' refund checks. A preparer faces a fine of $500 for each violation. ###

17. All the following statements regarding confidentiality protection for enrolled practitioners are correct except:

A. The protection relates to noncriminal tax matters before the IRS.
B. The protection applies to communications that would be considered privileged if they were between the taxpayer and an attorney.
C. The protection is granted to CPAs, enrolled agents, enrolled actuaries, and supervised preparers.
D. The protection is not granted in state tax proceedings.

The answer is C. The practitioner privilege is granted to attorneys, CPAs, enrolled agents, and enrolled actuaries, but not to supervised preparers. ###

18. Which statement is true regarding the privacy regulations in Internal Revenue Code §7216?

A. The regulations do not apply to e-file providers.
B. The improper disclosure must be "knowing or reckless" for criminal provisions to apply.
C. A practitioner may be fined up to $500 and imprisoned for up to one year for each violation of this code.
D. Tax practitioners must obtain oral consent from taxpayers before they can use information for anything other than the actual preparation of tax returns.

The answer is B. Internal Revenue Code §7216 is a criminal code that limits tax professionals' use and disclosure of client information. "B" is correct because criminal penalties will apply only if the improper disclosure is "knowing or reckless," rather than simply negligent. The other answers are incorrect because regulations do apply to e-file providers; a practitioner may be fined up to $1,000, not $500, and imprisoned for up to a year for each violation; and written consent, not oral, is generally required before taxpayer information can be disclosed. ###

19. How long must a tax professional retain records relating to clients who have offered their consent for representation in conflict-of-interest cases?

A. One year from the date representation ends.
B. Two years from the date representation ends.
C. Three years from the date representation ends.
D. Five years from the date representation ends.

The answer is C. In conflict of interest cases, a preparer must obtain consent in writing and retain the records for at least 36 months (three years) from the date representation ends. ###

20. In what situation is a return preparer allowed to disclose information without first obtaining written permission from a client?

A. When he is issued a subpoena by a state agency that regulates tax return preparers.
B. When he is contacted by a newspaper reporter investigating a possible crime committed by his client.
C. When the information is requested by his client's uncle who helps support the client financially.
D. When the information is needed by a preparer who volunteers with VITA.

The answer is A. A preparer who is issued a subpoena or court order, whether at the federal, state, or local level, is not required to obtain disclosure permission from a client. In all the other cases, disclosure is not allowed, unless there has been prior written consent. ###

21. Which designation or form gives the appointed person the greatest rights to represent a taxpayer?

A. Third party designee, also known as "Check Box" authority.
B. Form 8821, *Tax Information Authorization*.
C. Oral Tax Information authorization.
D. Form 2848, *Power of Attorney and Declaration of Representative.*

The answer is D. Only Form 2848, *Power of Attorney and Declaration of Representative,* allows a third party to represent a taxpayer before the IRS. The other consents are much more limited and allow only a third party to receive or inspect written or oral tax account information. ###

22. All of the following statements regarding a tax preparer's responsibility to provide information requested by the IRS are correct except:

A. He must promptly turn over all records relating to the IRS request, no matter what the circumstances.
B. If the records are not in his possession, he must make a "reasonable inquiry" of his client about their whereabouts.
C. He is not legally obligated to contact any third party who might possess the requested records.
D. If he believes in good faith and on reasonable grounds that the requested material is legally privileged information, a preparer may choose to decline a records request.

The answer is A. Although Circular 230 dictates that a return preparer comply promptly with information and record requests, there are limited circumstances when records do not have to be turned over. A preparer may decline to do so if he believes in good faith that the request is not legal or if the information is privileged. ###

23. In which instance is a tax preparer allowed to charge a contingent fee?

A. When his regular fee is "unconscionable."
B. When the fee is based on a claim for refund only.
C. When the IRS rules that a certain position taken on a return is not allowed.
D. When the preparer renders services in connection with an IRS court proceeding.

The answer is D. There are very strict rules for when preparers are permitted to charge contingent fees (percentage of a refund). Only in very limited instances are these fees allowed, such as when a preparer offers services in connection with any IRC-related litigation or judicial proceeding. ###

24. What penalty does a preparer face for failing to sign a client's claim for refund?

A. A warning letter from the IRS.
B. A fine of $50.
C. A fine of $100.
D. A fine of $500.

The answer is B. Under IRC §6695, the IRS lists the penalties that may be assessed when it comes to the preparation of tax returns for other persons. The penalty is $50 for each violation of the following:

1. Failure to furnish a copy of a return or claim to a taxpayer
2. Failure to sign a return or claim for refund
3. Failure to furnish an identifying number (PTIN) on a return
4. Failure to retain a copy or list of a return or claim
5. Failure to file correct information returns

A preparer faces a maximum penalty of $25,000 per calendar year or return period for these types of violations.
###

Unit 4: Taxpayer Obligations, Fraud, & Penalties

> **More Reading:**
> Publication 583, *Starting a Business and Keeping Records*
> Publication 552, *Recordkeeping for Individuals*
> Publication 947, *Practice Before the IRS and Power of Attorney*

Basic Recordkeeping Requirements

There are some basic recordkeeping requirements expected of U.S. taxpayers that tax preparers need to be familiar with and make sure their clients understand. Various types of recordkeeping requirements are tested on all three parts of the EA exam.

Part 3 of the EA exam focuses on the substantiation of items and records retention. There are also specific recordkeeping requirements relating to the Earned Income Credit that are tested on Part 3. (The due diligence requirements for EIC claims are covered later in Unit 5).

Except in a few cases, tax law does not require specific kinds of records to be kept. Any records that clearly demonstrate expenses, basis, and income should be retained. Generally, this means the taxpayer must keep records that support an item of income or deduction on a return until the statute of limitations for the tax return runs out. The IRS recommends that taxpayers keep all sales slips, invoices, receipts, canceled checks, or other financial account statements relating to a particular transaction.

A taxpayer may choose any recordkeeping system that clearly reflects income and expenses. He must keep records as long as they may be needed for the administration of any provision of the Internal Revenue Code.

If a taxpayer or business decides to use a computer recordkeeping system, he or the business must still retain a record of original documents. However, these documents may be scanned or kept on a computer imaging system. The IRS generally does not require a taxpayer to keep original paper records (Rev. Proc. 97-22).

Statute of Limitations for Records Retention

A taxpayer should keep all relevant records until the statute of limitations for his tax return expires. For assessment of tax owed, this period is generally three years from the date the return was filed or the return was due, whichever is later.

For filing a claim for credit or refund, the period to make the claim generally is three years from the date the original return was filed or two years from the date the tax was paid, whichever is later.

Records relating to the basis of property should be retained as long as they may be material to any tax return involving the property. The basis of property is material until the statute of limitations expires for the tax year an asset is sold or disposed of. A taxpayer must keep these records to figure any depreciation, amortization, or depletion deductions, and to figure the asset's basis.

Example: Cory has owned a vacation home for eight years, but in 2012 he decides to sell it. In order to compute basis and his gain on the property, he should have the records relating to the purchase of the property, and any other events that would add or subtract from his basis. He reports the sale of the vacation home on his 2012 tax return. He must continue to retain the records relating to the sale of the home until the statute of limitations for the tax return expires, usually three years from the date of filing or the due date of the return, whichever is later.

There are longer record retention periods in some cases. If a taxpayer files a claim from a loss of worthless securities, then the period to retain records related to the transaction is seven years.

If a taxpayer fails to report income that exceeds more than 25% of the gross income shown on his return, the statute of limitations is six years from when the return is filed. There is no statute of limitations to assess tax when a return is fraudulent or when no return is filed.

Recordkeeping for Employment (Payroll) Tax Returns

A business is required to retain payroll and employment tax records for at least four years after the tax becomes due or is paid, whichever is later. Examples include: copies of employees' income tax withholding allowance certificates (Forms W-4), records of fringe benefits provided, and dates and amounts of payroll tax deposits made. This rule also applies to businesses that employ other tax preparers.

> **Example:** Joelle is an EA who employs five other preparers in her office. She is required to keep the employment tax records relating to her employees for at least four years.

All employer tax records must be made available for IRS review. Necessary records include:

- Employer Identification Numbers (EIN)
- Amounts and dates of all wage, annuity, and pension payments, and amounts of tips reported (if applicable)
- The fair market value of in-kind wages paid
- Names, addresses, Social Security numbers, and occupations of employees and recipients
- Any copies of Form W-2 that were returned undeliverable
- Dates of active employment
- Periods for which employees were paid sick leave
- Copies of employees' and recipients' income tax withholding allowance certificates (Forms W-4)
- Dates and amounts of tax deposits
- Copies of all employment returns filed
- Records of fringe benefits provided, including substantiation

Statute of Limitations	
Type of Record/Return	**Minimum Retention Period**
Normal tax return	3 years
Omitted income that exceeds 25% of the gross income shown on the return	6 years
A fraudulent return	No limit
No return filed	No limit
A claim for credit or amended return	The later of 3 years or 2 years after tax was paid
A claim for a loss from worthless securities	7 years
Employment and payroll tax records	The later of 4 years after tax becomes due or is paid.
Fixed assets, Real estate	Records should be kept until after the expiration of the statute of limitations for the tax year in which the asset is sold or disposed of.

Test-takers should memorize these retention periods as they are often tested on the EA exam.

Tax Avoidance vs. Tax Evasion

The term "tax avoidance" is not defined by the IRS, but it is commonly used to describe the legal reduction of taxable income. Most taxpayers use at least a few methods of tax avoidance in order to reduce their taxable income and therefore lower their tax liability.

Example: Nate contributes to his employer-sponsored retirement plans with pretax funds. He also uses an employer-based Flexible Spending Account for his medical expenses, which reduces his taxable income by making all of his medical expenses pretax. Nate is using *legal* tax avoidance in order to reduce his taxable income.

Tax *evasion*, on the other hand, is an illegal practice in which individuals or businesses intentionally avoid paying their true tax liability. All citizens must comply with tax law. Although most Americans recognize their civic duty and comply with their tax obligations, the U.S. government estimates that approximately 3% of taxpayers do not file tax returns at all. Those caught evading taxes are subject to criminal charges and substantial penalties.

For each year a taxpayer does not file a return, the penalty can include a fine of up to $25,000 and a prison sentence of up to one year. If it can be demonstrated that the taxpayer deliberately did not file in an attempt to evade taxation, the IRS can pursue a felony conviction, which could include a fine of up to $100,000 and a maximum prison sentence of five years.

Exam takers should be familiar with the specifics of each of these penalties, as well as others detailed in this unit.

Penalties Imposed Upon Taxpayers

For individual taxpayers, the IRS can assess a penalty for those who fail to file, fail to pay, or both. The failure-to-file penalty is generally greater than the failure-to-pay penalty. If someone is unable to pay all the taxes he owes, he is better off filing on time and paying as much as he can. The IRS will explore payment options with individual taxpayers.

Failure-to-file Penalty

The penalty for filing late is usually 5% of the unpaid taxes for each month or part of a month that a return is late. This penalty will not exceed 25% of a taxpayer's unpaid taxes. The penalty is based on the tax not paid by the due date, without regard to extensions.

If a taxpayer files his return more than 60 days after the due date or extended due date, the minimum penalty is the smaller of $135 or 100% of the unpaid tax. If the taxpayer is owed a refund, there will not be a failure-to-file penalty.[29]

Failure-to-pay Penalty

If a taxpayer does not pay his taxes by the due date, he will be subject to a failure-to-pay penalty of ½ of 1% (0.5%) of unpaid taxes for each month or part of a month after the due date that the taxes are not paid. This penalty can be as much as 25% of a taxpayer's unpaid taxes.

If a taxpayer filed for an extension of time to file by the tax deadline and he paid at least 90% of his actual tax liability by the original due date, he will not face a failure-to-pay penalty so long as the remaining balance is paid by the extended due date.

The failure-to-pay penalty rate increases to a full 1% per month for any tax that remains unpaid the day after a demand for immediate payment is issued, or ten days after notice of intent to levy certain assets is issued. For taxpayers who filed on time but are unable to pay their tax liabilities, the failure-to-pay penalty rate is reduced to ¼ of 1% (0.25%) per month during any month in which the taxpayer has a valid installment agreement with the IRS.

If both the failure-to-file penalty and the failure-to-pay penalty apply in any month, the 5% failure-to-file penalty is reduced by the failure-to-pay penalty. However, if a taxpayer files his return more than 60 days after the due date or extended

---

[29] Please note that the rules regarding failure-to-file penalties are different for entities (corporations, partnerships, trusts, etc.) In the case of partnerships and corporations, a late filing penalty may apply even if the entity shows a loss, or does not owe any tax.

due date, the minimum penalty remains the smaller of $135 or 100% of the unpaid tax.

A taxpayer will not have to pay either penalty if he shows he failed to file or pay on time because of reasonable cause and not willful neglect.

Penalties are payable upon notice and demand. Penalties are generally assessed, collected, and paid in the same manner as taxes. The taxpayer will receive a notice that contains:

- The name of the penalty,
- The applicable code section, and
- How the penalty was computed.

Accuracy-Related Penalties

The two most common accuracy-related penalties are the "substantial understatement" penalty and the "negligence or disregard of regulations" penalty. These penalties are calculated as a flat 20% of the net understatement of tax. In addition to other penalties, if the taxpayer provides fraudulent information on his tax return, he can be subject to a civil fraud penalty.

Penalty for Substantial Understatement

The understatement is considered "substantial" if it is more than the larger of:

- 10% of the correct tax, or

- $5,000 for individuals.

A taxpayer may avoid the substantial understatement penalty if he has substantial authority (such as previous court cases) for his position or through adequate disclosure.

To avoid the substantial understatement penalty by adequate disclosure, the taxpayer (or tax preparer) must properly disclose the position on the tax return and there must be at least a reasonable basis for the position.

Trust Fund Recovery Penalty (TFRP)

The trust fund recovery penalty is most commonly exacted on employers. It is also called the "100% penalty" because the IRS will assess a tax of 100% of the amount due.

As authorized by IRC Section 6672, this penalty involves the income and Social Security taxes an employer withholds from the wages of employees. These taxes are called "trust fund" taxes because they are held in trust for the government. They have been withheld from an employee's paycheck, so the employer is required to remit them to the IRS. Sometimes, when business owners have financial trouble, they neglect to remit these taxes to the IRS.

The trust fund recovery penalty can be assessed against anyone who is considered a "responsible person" in the business. This includes corporate officers, directors, stockholders, and even rank-and-file employees. The IRS has assessed the penalty against accountants, bookkeepers, or even clerical staff, particularly if they have authority to sign checks. In determining whether to proceed with assertion of the TFRP, the IRS must determine:

- Responsibility, and
- Willfulness.

A person must be both "responsible" and "willful" to be liable for an employer's failure to collect or pay trust fund taxes to the United States. This means that he knew (or should have known) that the payroll taxes were not being remitted to the IRS, and that he also had the power to correct the problem. Usually, this means that the individual had check-signing authority, but each case is evaluated by the IRS.

Example: Shelly works for Wilsonville Construction as a full-time bookkeeper and processes all the payroll tax forms. She also has check-signing authority, so she can pay the bills when her boss is working off-site. In 2012, her boss has a heart attack, and his wife, Doreen, takes over the business in his absence. Doreen can't manage the business properly and Wilsonville Construction soon falls into debt. Doreen tells Shelly to pay vendors first. The business continues to withhold payroll taxes from employee paychecks, but does not remit the amounts to the IRS. Eventually, the business goes under and Doreen disappears. Shelly is contacted by the IRS shortly thereafter. Even though Shelly was "just an employee," the IRS can assess the trust fund recovery penalty against her because (1) she had check-signing authority, and (2) she knew that the business was not lawfully remitting payroll taxes to the IRS as required.

The trust fund recovery penalty may be assessed *in addition* to any other penalties, including the failure-to-file, failure-to-pay, or fraud penalties.

Other Penalties

Civil Fraud Penalty

If there is any underpayment of tax due to fraud, a penalty of 75% of the underpayment will be assessed against the taxpayer. The fraud penalty on a joint return does not automatically apply to a spouse unless some part of the under-payment is due to the fraud of that spouse. The injured spouse may request relief from joint liability in this case.

Negligence or simple ignorance of the law does not constitute fraud. Typically, IRS examiners who find strong evidence of fraud will refer the case to the IRS Criminal Investigation Division for possible criminal prosecution.

Frivolous and Fraudulent Returns

Some Americans assert that they are not required to file federal tax returns or pay federal tax because they claim that our system of taxation is based upon voluntary assessment and payment. These arguments are considered "frivolous positions."

Some tax protesters maintain that there is no federal statute imposing a tax on income derived from sources within the U.S. by citizens or residents of the United States. They argue instead that federal income taxes are excise taxes imposed only on nonresident aliens and foreign corporations for the privilege of receiving income from sources within the United States.

In addition to tax protesters, there are many other ways taxpayers attempt to defraud the government by not paying their tax liability. All of the following are illegal schemes, and anyone participating in them or promoting them can be liable for civil and criminal penalties:

- Abusive home-based business schemes
- Abusive trust schemes
- Misuse of the disabled access credit
- Abusive offshore bank schemes
- Exempt organizations' abusive tax avoidance transactions

Failure to Supply Social Security Number

If a taxpayer does not include a Social Security Number or the SSN of another person where required on a return, statement, or other document, he will be subject to a penalty of $50 for each failure. The taxpayer will also be subject to the $50 penalty if he does not give the SSN to another person when it is required on a return, statement, or other document.

Any taxpayer who files a tax return that is considered "frivolous" may have to pay a penalty of $5,000, *in addition* to any other penalty provided by law. This penalty may be doubled on a joint return. A taxpayer will be subject to this penalty if he files a tax return based simply on the desire to interfere with the administration of tax law.

The IRS takes fraudulent returns very seriously. Should a taxpayer choose to participate in a fraudulent tax scheme, he will not be shielded from potential civil and criminal sanctions, regardless of whether or not he used a tax preparer.

A "fraudulent return" also includes a return in which the individual is attempting to file using someone else's name or SSN, or when the taxpayer is presenting documents or information that have no basis in fact.

A potentially abusive return also includes a return that contains inaccurate information that may lead to an understatement of a liability or the overstatement of a credit resulting in a refund to which the taxpayer is not entitled.

Alteration of the Jurat is Prohibited and Considered Frivolous

Some taxpayers attempt to reduce their federal tax liability by striking out the written declaration, known as the "jurat," that verifies a return is made under penalties of perjury.

The Jurat

> **Example:** A taxpayer files Form 1040 for the 2012 tax year. The taxpayer signs the form but crosses out the jurat on the return and writes the word "void" across it. This return is now considered "frivolous" and is subject to penalties.

Civil penalties for altering a jurat include:

- A $500 penalty imposed under Section 6702;
- Additional penalties for failure to file a return, failure to pay tax owed, and fraudulent failure to file a return; and
- A penalty of up to $25,000 under Section 6673 if the taxpayer makes frivolous arguments in the United States Tax Court.

Client Fraud

The IRS encourages tax preparers to look for client fraud. Sometimes, the taxpayer is merely negligent or careless, or may have an honest difference of opinion regarding the deductibility of an expense. If fraud is actually taking place, there are some common "badges of fraud" that the IRS looks for. Examples include:

- The understatement of income or improper deductions
- Personal items deducted as business expenses
- The overstatement of deductions or taking improper credits
- Making false entries in documents or destroying records
- Not cooperating with the IRS or avoiding IRS contact
- Concealing or transferring assets
- Engaging in illegal activity
- Sloppy recordkeeping
- All-cash businesses

Some of these actions taken by themselves do not necessarily constitute fraud. However, consistent abuses or multiple red flags may be a reason to suspect taxpayer fraud.

Tax Practitioner Fraud

Tax professionals are sometimes guilty of preparer fraud. Preparer fraud generally involves the preparation and filing of false income tax returns with inflated personal or business expenses, false deductions, unallowable credits, or excessive exemptions on returns prepared for their clients. Preparers may also manipulate income figures to obtain fraudulent tax credits, such as the Earned Income Credit.

The preparers' clients may or may not know about the false expenses, deductions, exemptions and/or credits shown on their tax returns. Fraudulent preparers gain financially by:

- Diverting a portion of the refund for their own benefit;
- Increasing their clientele by developing a reputation for obtaining large refunds; and/or
- Charging inflated fees for the return preparation.

Preparer Penalties for Preparing Fraudulent Returns

All paid preparers are subject to civil penalties for actions ranging from knowingly preparing a return that understates the taxpayer's liability to failing to sign or provide an identification number on a return they prepare. Tax return preparers who demonstrate a pattern of misconduct may be banned from preparing further returns. Additionally, the IRS may pursue and impose criminal penalties against a tax return preparer who engages in severe misconduct.

For the purpose of preparer penalties, a preparer may rely in good faith upon information furnished by the taxpayer or a previous preparer, and is not required to independently verify or review the items reported on tax returns to determine if they are likely to be upheld if challenged by the IRS.

However, a preparer must make "reasonable inquiries" if the information appears to be incorrect or incomplete. A tax return preparer is not considered to have complied with the "good faith" requirements if:

- The advice is unreasonable on its face;
- He knew or should have known that the third party advisor was not aware of all relevant facts; or
- He knew or should have known (given the nature of the tax return preparer's practice) at the time the tax return or claim for refund was prepared, that the advice was no longer reliable due to developments in the law since the time the advice was given.

Example: Martin is an EA who conducts an interview with his client, Barbara. She states she made a $50,000 charitable contribution of real estate during the tax year when in fact she did not make this charitable contribution. Martin does not inquire about the existence of a qualified appraisal or complete Form 8283 in accordance with reporting and substantiation requirements. Martin reports a deduction for the charitable contribution, which results in an understatement of tax liability. Barbara's return is later audited, and the charitable deduction is disallowed. Because of his negligence, Martin is subject to a preparer penalty under Section 6694.

Example: Allie is an enrolled agent. She prepares her client's 2012 tax return and discovers certain expenses that are not deductible. However, the previous year, there was one District Court case where the court ruled in favor of the taxpayer, allowing the taxpayer to claim similar expenses. No other court cases are currently being litigated, and the IRS has not issued a statement of opinion on the case. Based on these facts, Allie will have a reasonable basis for claiming the expenses on her client's 2012 return. Allie will not be subject to the Section 6694 penalty as long as the position is adequately disclosed, because the position has a legal justification as a challenge to the current IRS position.

If a preparer willfully understates a client's tax liability, he is subject to penalties. Under IRS regulations, "understatement of liability" means:

- Understating net tax payable
- Overstating the net amount creditable or refundable
- Taking a position with no realistic possibility of success

Penalties for Understatement of Taxpayer Liability

There are two specific penalties when an income tax preparer understates a taxpayer's liability.

Understatement Due to an Unrealistic Position: If there is an understatement on a tax return due to an unrealistic position, the penalty is the greater of:

- $1,000 per tax return, or
- 50% of the additional income upon which the penalty was imposed.

This applies when a preparer knows, or reasonably should have known, that the position was unrealistic and would not have been sustained on its merits. However, if the position is adequately disclosed on a tax return, this penalty will not apply. In the case of a patently frivolous position (such as a tax protester position), the penalty will apply whether or not it is disclosed. A preparer may be excused from the penalty if he acted in good faith and there was reasonable cause for the understatement.

Understatement Due to Negligent or Willful Disregard: If a tax preparer shows negligent or willful disregard of IRS rules and regulations, and makes a willful or reckless attempt to understate tax liability, the penalty is the greater of:

- $5,000 per tax return, or
- 50% of the additional income upon which the penalty was imposed.

If a tax preparer is subject to a penalty for understatement of liability and this includes a change to the Earned Income Credit, then the preparer may be subject to additional penalties for failure to exercise due diligence while claiming the EIC.

A tax preparer may avoid these harsh penalties if he relied on the advice of another preparer in good faith. The penalty may also be avoided if the position is adequately disclosed on a tax return and is not frivolous. In this case, a tax preparer would bear the burden of proof.

Abusive Tax Shelter: Any tax preparer who organizes, sells, or promotes an abusive tax shelter will be subject to penalties of $1,000 for each activity, or 100% of the gross income derived from the activity, whichever is less.

Penalty Abatement

If a penalty is assessed against a tax preparer and he does not agree with the assessment, he may request a conference with the IRS officer or agent and explain why the penalty is not warranted. The preparer may also wait for the penalty to be assessed, pay the penalty within 30 days, and then file a claim for refund.

IRC Section 6694 states that the understatement penalty will be abated if, under final judicial decision, it is found that there is no actual understatement of liability. Sometimes this will occur when a tax court case is decided in favor of the taxpayer.

The Office of Professional Responsibility

As reorganized under the revisions to Circular 230, the OPR's mission is to "support effective tax administration by ensuring all tax practitioners, tax preparers, and other third parties in the tax system adhere to professional standards and follow the law."

Specifically, the OPR has the authority to exercise responsibility for all matters related to practitioner conduct, discipline, and practice before the IRS. This authority includes:

- Receiving and processing referrals regarding allegations of misconduct under Circular 230; initiating all disciplinary proceedings against individuals or entities relating to allegations or findings of practitioner misconduct consistent with the applicable disciplinary rules under Circular 230.

- Making final determinations on appeal from return preparer eligibility or suitability decisions; recommending and imposing all sanctions for violations under Circular 230 and accepting consents to be sanctioned under the same.
- Making determinations on whether to appeal administrative law judge decisions and reviewing and determining petitions seeking reinstatement to practice. [30]

Disciplinary Sanctions Against Practitioners

The OPR may impose a wide range of sanctions upon preparers:

Disbarment from practice before the IRS— An individual who is disbarred is not eligible to represent taxpayers before the IRS. Also, as a result of a suspension or disbarment, the practitioner will have his PTIN revoked.

Suspension from practice before the IRS— An individual who is suspended is not eligible to represent taxpayers before the IRS during the term of the suspension.

Censure in practice before the IRS— Censure is a public reprimand. Unlike disbarment or suspension, censure does not affect an individual's eligibility to represent taxpayers before the IRS, but the OPR may subject the individual's future representations to conditions designed to promote high standards of conduct.

Monetary penalty— A monetary penalty may be imposed on an individual who engages in conduct subject to sanction or on an employer, firm, or entity if the individual was acting on its behalf and if it knew, or reasonably should have known, of the individual's conduct. This fine may be in addition to or in lieu of any suspension, disbarment, or censure.

Disqualification of appraiser— An appraiser who is disqualified is barred from presenting evidence or testimony in any administrative proceeding before the Department of the Treasury or the IRS.

Preparer Incompetence and Disreputable Conduct

Circular 230 outlines many instances in which a practitioner might be sanctioned for disreputable or incompetent representation. These instances include:
- Conviction of any criminal offense under federal tax laws.
- Conviction of any criminal offense involving dishonesty or breach of trust.

---

[30] IRS Delegation Order 25-16, July 16, 2012.

- Conviction of any felony under federal or state law in which the conduct renders the practitioner unfit to practice before the IRS.
- Giving false or misleading information, or participating in any way in the giving of false or misleading information to the Department of the Treasury.
- Soliciting employment as prohibited under Circular 230 or making false or misleading representations with intent to deceive a client.
- Willfully failing to file a federal tax return, or willfully evading any assessment or payment of any federal tax.
- Willfully assisting a client in violating any federal tax law, or knowingly counseling a client to evade federal taxes.
- Misappropriating funds received from a client for the purpose of payment of taxes.
- Attempting to influence any IRS officer by the use of threats, false accusations, duress, coercion, or bribery.
- Disbarment or suspension from practice as an attorney, CPA, or actuary. (For example, if a CPA is disbarred at the state level, he would also be disbarred at the federal level).
- Knowingly aiding and abetting another person to practice before the IRS during a period of suspension, disbarment, or ineligibility of such other person.
- Contemptuous conduct in connection with practice before the IRS, including the use of abusive language, making accusations or statements knowing them to be false, or circulating or publishing malicious or libelous matter.
- Giving a false opinion knowingly, recklessly, or through gross incompetence.
- Willfully disclosing or using private tax return information; willfully failing to sign a tax return; willfully failing to e-file a return; willfully signing a tax return without a valid PTIN; and willfully representing a taxpayer before the IRS without appropriate authorization.

The IRS may sanction a practitioner for any of these violations, or for engaging in "reckless conduct." This is defined as an "extreme departure from the standards" a practitioner should normally observe. The IRS will look at a practitioner's pattern of conduct to see whether it reflects gross incompetence, meaning "gross indifference, preparation which is grossly inadequate under the circumstances, and a consistent failure to perform obligations to the client."

Judicial Proceedings for Preparer Misconduct

There are four broad categories of preparer misconduct, all of which may be subject to disciplinary action:

- Misconduct while representing a taxpayer
- Misconduct related to the practitioner's own return
- Giving a false opinion, knowingly, recklessly, or through gross incompetence
- Misconduct not directly involving IRS representation (such as a felony conviction)

The Secretary of the Treasury, after notice and an opportunity for a proceeding, may censure, suspend, or disbar any practitioner from practice before the IRS for misconduct.

A practitioner who is disbarred may not practice before the IRS. A practitioner who is suspended may not practice during the period of the suspension.

A practitioner who is listed as "inactive status" or "retirement status" may not practice before the IRS.

Inactive retirement status is not available to an individual who is the subject of a pending disciplinary matter.

Example: Tim is a CPA who was disbarred by his state society and his license revoked for a felony conviction not related to his tax practice. Even though his CPA license was revoked for a separate issue, the OPR still considers this disreputable conduct. Since Tim has been stripped of his license, he is not enrolled to practice before the IRS. He can be permanently disbarred or censured by the OPR.

Conferences and Voluntary Consents

If the OPR has evidence or allegations of misconduct, the director of the OPR may confer with the practitioner, employer, firm, or other party concerning the allegations. A formal proceeding does not have to be instituted in order for the OPR to confer with other parties regarding the alleged misconduct.

A practitioner may offer consent to be sanctioned *in lieu of* a formal proceeding. The director of the OPR may, in his discretion, accept or decline the practitioner's consent to a sanction. The director may accept a revised offer submitted in response to his rejection or may counteroffer and act upon any accepted counter-offer.

Complaints Against a Tax Practitioner

The OPR can issue a formal complaint against a practitioner. In order to be valid, a complaint must:

- Name the respondent.
- Provide a clear and concise description of the facts.
- Be signed by the director of the OPR.
- Describe the type of sanction.

A complaint is considered sufficient if it informs the respondent of the charges so that the respondent is able to prepare a defense.

The OPR must notify the practitioner of the deadline for answering the complaint. The deadline may not be less than 30 days from the date of service of the complaint. The OPR must also give the name and address of the administrative law judge with whom the response must be filed, and the name and address of the employee representing the OPR.

Service of Complaint Against a Tax Practitioner

The complaint may be served to the practitioner in the following ways: Certified mail, First Class mail if returned undelivered by Certified mail; private delivery service; in person; or by leaving the complaint at the office of the practitioner. Electronic delivery, such as e-mail, is not a valid means of serving a complaint.

Within ten days of serving the complaint, copies of the evidence against the practitioner must also be served. The practitioner must respond to the complaint by the deadline outlined in the letter. A failure to respond constitutes an admission of guilt and a waiver of the hearing.

An administrative law judge is the one who will actually hear the evidence and decide whether the OPR has proven its case against a practitioner. If the practitioner fails to respond to the complaint, the administrative law judge may make a decision on the case by default without a hearing.

During a hearing, the practitioner may appear in person or be represented by an attorney or another practitioner. The director of the OPR may be represented by an attorney or other employee of the IRS.

If either party to the judicial proceeding fails to appear at the hearing, the absent party shall be deemed to have waived the right to a hearing, and the administrative law judge may make his decision against the absent party by default.

Within 180 days from the conclusion of a hearing, the administrative law judge should enter a decision in the case. He must provide a copy of his decision to the director of the OPR and to the practitioner or to the practitioner's authorized representative.

If there is no appeal, the decision becomes final. However, either party—the OPR or the practitioner—may appeal the judge's decision with the Secretary of the Treasury within 30 days. The Secretary of the Treasury, or his delegate, will then make a final determination on the case.

Disbarment vs. Suspension

When the final decision in a judicial proceeding is for disbarment, the practitioner will not be allowed to practice in any capacity before the IRS (except to represent himself). A disbarred practitioner may not:

- Prepare or file documents, including tax returns, or other correspondence with the IRS. The restriction applies regardless of whether the individual signs the document and regardless of whether the individual personally files or directs another person to file, documents with the IRS.
- Render written advice with respect to any entity, transaction, plan or arrangement having a potential for tax avoidance or evasion (tax shelter advice).
- Represent a client at conferences, hearings, and meetings.
- Execute waivers, consents, or closing agreements; receive a taxpayer's refund check; or sign a tax return on behalf of a taxpayer.
- File powers of attorney with the IRS.
- Accept assistance from another person (or request assistance) or assist another person (or offer assistance) if the assistance relates to a matter constituting practice before the IRS, or enlist another person for the purpose of practicing before the IRS.
- State or imply that he is eligible to practice before the IRS.

However, a suspended or disbarred individual is still allowed to:

- Represent himself in any matter.[31]
- Appear before the IRS as a trustee, receiver, guardian, administrator, executor, or other fiduciary if duly qualified/authorized under the law of the relevant jurisdiction.[32]
- Appear as a witness for the taxpayer.[33]
- Furnish information at the request of the IRS or any of its officers or employees.[34]

A practitioner may petition the OPR for reinstatement after a period of five years. The OPR may reinstate the practitioner if it determines that his conduct is not likely to be in violation of regulations and if granting the reinstatement is not contrary to the public interest.

---

[31]Authorized under Section 10.7(a).

[32] Authorized under Section 10.7(e). Fiduciaries should file Form 56, *Notice Concerning Fiduciary Relationship.*

[33] Authorized under Section 10.8(b) and Revenue Procedure 68-29, reprinted in pamphlet form as Publication 499.

[34]Authorized under Section 10.8(b)

Unit 4: Questions

1. Which of the following is true?

A. The IRS may not disbar a preparer without first seeking a legal criminal prosecution.
B. Even without bringing a criminal prosecution, the IRS may choose to disbar a tax return preparer.
C. A preparer is not liable for any preparer penalties if he diverts a portion of the refund to himself with the client's permission.
D. None of the above.

The answer is B. Even without bringing a criminal prosecution, the IRS may choose to disbar or prevent a tax return preparer from engaging in specific abusive practices. ###

2. What types of behavior would not subject a tax practitioner to be sanctioned by the OPR?

A. Misconduct while representing a taxpayer.
B. Misconduct related to the practitioner's own return.
C. When the practitioner is unable to pay his personal taxes due.
D. Misconduct not directly involving IRS representation.

The answer is C. Not being able to pay one's taxes on time would, most likely, not subject a tax practitioner to OPR sanctions. In general, the OPR defines four broad categories of misconduct, which may be subject to disciplinary action: (1) misconduct while representing a taxpayer; (2) misconduct related to the practitioner's own return; (3) giving a false opinion, knowingly, recklessly, or through gross incompetence; (4) misconduct not directly involving IRS representation. ###

3. All of the following statements regarding the fraud penalty are correct except:

A. If there is any underpayment of tax due to fraud, a penalty of 75% of the underpayment will be assessed against the taxpayer.
B. The fraud penalty on a joint return will automatically apply to a spouse.
C. IRS examiners who find strong evidence of fraud may refer the case to the IRS Criminal Investigation Division for possible criminal prosecution.
D. Negligence or simple ignorance of the law does not constitute fraud.

The answer is B. The fraud penalty on a joint return does not automatically apply to a spouse unless some part of the underpayment is due to the fraud of that spouse. ###

4. Glen is a CPA who prepares income tax returns for his clients. One of his clients submits a list of expenses to be claimed on Schedule C of the return. Glen qualifies as a return preparer and, as such, is required to comply with which one of the following conditions?

A. Glen is required to independently verify the client's information.
B. Glen can ignore implications of information known by him.
C. Inquiry is not required if the information appears to be incorrect or incomplete.
D. Appropriate inquiries are required to determine whether the client has substantiation for travel and entertainment expenses.

The answer is D. The preparer is not required to independently examine evidence of deductions. A preparer may rely in good faith without verification upon information furnished by the taxpayer if it does not appear to be incorrect or incomplete. However, the tax preparer must make reasonable inquiries about the validity of the information. ###

5. Which of the following types of disciplinary actions allow a practitioner to continue practicing before the IRS?

A. Disbarment.
B. Suspension from practice.
C. Public censure.
D. All of the disciplinary actions listed above will prevent a practitioner from practicing before the IRS.

The answer is C. A practitioner who is censured by the OPR is still eligible to practice before the IRS. Censure is a public reprimand. Unlike disbarment or suspension, censure does not affect an individual's eligibility to represent taxpayers before the IRS, but the OPR may subject the individual's future representations to conditions designed to promote high standards of conduct. ###

6. Melissa, an EA, was notified of a judicial ruling that she committed acts of gross misconduct and violated the rules of Circular 230, and, therefore, a decision was entered that she should be disbarred. Which of the following is true?

A. Melissa has a right to appeal the decision to the Secretary of the Treasury.
B. Melissa has a right to appeal the decision to the Office of Professional Responsibility.
C. Melissa has a right to appeal the decision to the Return Preparer Office.
D. Melissa has a right to appeal the decision to the Commissioner of the IRS.

The answer is A. An enrolled agent has a right to appeal the decision for disbarment to the Secretary of the Treasury. ###

7. Mario, an EA, prepared a client's tax return that contained a frivolous position which could not be defended under any circumstances. The examiner who conducted the examination made a referral to the Office of Professional Responsibility. After all procedural requirements have been met, who will make the final decision as to the appropriate sanction for Mario?

A. The OPR.
B. An administrative law judge.
C. IRS legal counsel.
D. The IRS examination division.

The answer is B. The OPR investigates complaints against preparers and then institutes judicial proceedings. However, if a hearing is required, an administrative law judge will make the decision regarding disbarment or other appropriate sanctions. ###

8. What types of sanctions will not be imposed by the OPR?

A. Disbarment.
B. Suspension.
C. Incarceration.
D. Censure.

The answer is C. OPR sanctions include disbarment, suspension, and censure. Although a tax preparer may be subject to criminal prosecution in some cases, the OPR would not be responsible for applying this penalty. ###

9. Following a disbarment, a tax practitioner may petition the OPR for reinstatement after a period of _____.

A. One year.
B. Five years.
C. Ten years.
D. Never. Disbarment is always permanent.

The answer is B. A practitioner may petition the OPR for reinstatement after a period of five years. ###

10. A suspended or disbarred individual may:

A. Appear before the IRS as a trustee, receiver, guardian, administrator, executor, or other fiduciary if duly authorized under the law of the relevant jurisdiction.
B. File documents on a taxpayer's behalf.
C. Represent a client at conferences, hearings, and meetings.
D. Execute a closing agreement for a client, so long as the practitioner has a valid power of attorney.

The answer is A. A disbarred practitioner may appear before the IRS as a trustee, receiver, guardian, administrator, executor, or other fiduciary if duly qualified/authorized under the law of the relevant jurisdiction. This is authorized under Section 10.7(e). Fiduciaries should file Form 56, *Notice Concerning Fiduciary Relationship*. ###

11. Carlos owns a business with three employees. How long is Carlos required to keep payroll tax records?

A. Three years.
B. Four years.
C. Six years.
D. Seven years.

The answer is B. A taxpayer or business is required to keep records relating to employment taxes for at least four years after filing the fourth quarter for the year. Employment and payroll records must be available for IRS review. Examples include copies of employees' income tax withholding allowance certificates (Forms W-4), and dates and amounts of payroll tax deposits made. ###

12. If there is substantial unreported income (over 25%), the IRS may audit tax returns for up to _____ after the filing date.

A. Three years.
B. Four years.
C. Six years.
D. Indefinitely.

The answer is C. In most cases, tax returns can be audited for up to three years after filing. However, the IRS may audit for up to six years if there is substantial unreported income (over 25% omitted). ###

13. Records for claim of loss from a worthless security should be kept for:

A. Three years.
B. Four years.
C. Six years.
D. Seven years.

The answer is D. Records relating to a claim for a loss from worthless securities should be kept for seven years. That is because a taxpayer can file an amended return to take a loss on a worthless security up to seven years after the filing date. ###

14. Colleen owns a business and has never filed a tax return. How long should she keep her records?

A. Three years if she owes additional tax.
B. Seven years if she files a claim for a loss from worthless securities.
C. For an unlimited period of time if she does not file a return.
D. None of the above.

The answer is C. A taxpayer must keep records as long as they are needed for the administration of any provision of the IRC. Taxpayers must keep records that support an item of income or deduction on a tax return until the period of limitations for that return runs out. If a tax return is not filed, there is no time limit. ###

15. All of the following statements are correct except:

A. If no other provisions apply, the statute of limitations for an IRS examination of a return is three years after the return was filed or the return was due, whichever is later.
B. If more than 25% of gross income has been omitted from the tax return, the statute of limitations is six years after the return was filed.
C. If a fraudulent return is filed, the statute of limitations is seven years.
D. If a tax return is not filed at all, there is no statute of limitations.

The answer is C. If a fraudulent tax return is filed, there is NO statute of limitations for collection. Under federal law, a tax return is "fraudulent" if the taxpayer files it knowing that the return either omits taxable income or claims one or more deductions that are not allowable. ###

16. Which of the following statements is true?
A. Tax avoidance and tax evasion are always illegal.
B. Taxpayers who commit fraud are subject to civil penalties only.
C. The IRS will assess a failure-to-file penalty or a failure-to-pay penalty but never both.
D. A felony conviction against a taxpayer who deliberately failed to file taxes could mean a fine of up to $100,000 and a prison sentence of up to five years.

The answer is D. It is correct that this is the maximum penalty and prison sentence in a tax evasion case. The other statements are false—tax avoidance is not illegal; taxpayers who commit fraud are subject to criminal penalties in addition to civil ones; and the IRS may assess both failure-to-file and failure-to-pay penalties. ###

17. What is the minimum penalty for failing to file a tax return more than 60 days late (assuming the taxpayer is not owed a refund)?

A. 10% of the unpaid tax.
B. $135.
C. The smaller of $135 or 100% of the unpaid tax.
D. A minimum of 25% of a taxpayer's unpaid tax.

The answer is C. The minimum penalty is the smaller of $135 or 100% of the unpaid tax. ###

18. Under IRS rules, which penalty is worse: failure-to-file or failure-to-pay?

A. The failure-to-file penalty.
B. The failure-to-pay penalty.
C. Both have the same penalties.
D. None of the above.

The answer is A. The penalty for filing late is usually 5% of the unpaid taxes for each month that a return is late. The penalty for not paying taxes by the due date is less—½ of 1% (0.5%). The IRS advises that if someone is unable to pay all the taxes he owes, he is better off filing on time and paying as much as he can. ###

19. What percentage of tax must a taxpayer pay if he is guilty of a "substantial understatement" penalty?

A. 5% of the net understatement of tax.
B. 10% of the net understatement of tax.
C. 20% of the net understatement of tax.
D. 25% of the net understatement of tax.

The answer is C. The substantial understatement penalty is calculated as a flat 20% of the net understatement of tax. A taxpayer may also face additional fraud-related penalties if he has provided false information on his tax return. ###

20. All of the following statements about the trust fund recovery penalty are correct except:

A. This is also referred to as the "100% penalty."
B. The IRS targets employees for this penalty.
C. This penalty involves payroll taxes withheld from the wages of employees.
D. The penalty can be assessed against anyone who is considered a "responsible person" and has failed to collect or pay trust fund taxes to the U.S. government.

The answer is B. This penalty is generally levied against employers, not employees, who have failed to pay the appropriate payroll taxes to the U.S. government. ###

21. What is the penalty for a taxpayer who has filed a return that is considered "frivolous"?

A. $500, plus any other penalty provided by law.
B. $1,000, plus any other penalty provided by law.
C. $5,000, plus any other penalty provided by law.
D. $10,000, plus any other penalty provided by law.

The answer is C. Any taxpayer who files a return found to be "frivolous" may be fined $5,000, in addition to any other penalty provided by law. This penalty may be doubled on a joint return. ###

22. What is not considered a potential "badge of fraud" by the IRS?

A. Sloppy recordkeeping.
B. Taking improper credits.
C. All-cash businesses.
D. Deductions for foreign travel.

The answer is D. IRS auditors are trained to spot common types of deception and attempts to defraud on tax returns. These acts are known as badges of fraud, and include deducting personal items as business expenses, the overstatement of deductions, and the understatement of income. Simply having deductions for foreign travel is not an indication of illegal behavior on the part of a taxpayer. ###

23. What is the penalty a preparer faces for understating income on a tax return due to an unrealistic position?

A. $1,000 per tax return or 50% of the additional income upon which the penalty was imposed.
B. $5,000 per tax return.
C. 50% of the understatement.
D. Nothing, so long as the preparer fails to adequately disclose the position on the return.

The answer is A. A preparer faces an understatement penalty of $1,000 per tax return or 50% of the additional income upon which the penalty was imposed. However, if the position is adequately disclosed on the return, the penalty will not apply. ###

24. All of the following statements regarding preparer penalties are correct except:

A. A preparer who has been assessed a penalty may request a conference with an IRS officer to dispute the fine.
B. A preparer who makes a "willful or reckless" attempt to understate tax liability faces a fine of $10,000 per return.
C. There may be additional penalties for understatement of income if the preparer has not exercised due diligence related to the EIC.
D. A tax preparer may avoid penalties if he relied on the advice of another preparer in good faith.

The answer is B. A preparer who makes a "willful or reckless" attempt to understate tax liability faces a penalty of $5,000 per tax return or 50% of the additional income upon which the penalty was imposed, whichever is greater. ###

Unit 5: The Ethics of the EIC

> **More Reading:**
> **www.eitc.irs.gov**
> Publication 596, *Earned Income Credit*
> Publication 4687, *EITC Due Diligence Requirements*
> Publication 4808, *Disability and EITC*

Earned Income Credit Extra Due Diligence Requirements

The Earned Income Credit (EIC)[35] is a refundable federal income tax credit for low to moderate income working individuals and families. When the EIC exceeds the amount of taxes owed, it results in a tax refund to those who claim and qualify for the credit.

The due diligence rules for tax preparers are more stringent for EIC returns. The number of individuals claiming the EIC is high, and the number of erroneous claims is also high. The IRS estimates an error rate of 21 to 26%, or $15 billion paid out in error in 2011.

Paid preparers must meet four additional due diligence requirements on returns with EIC claims or face possible penalties. IRS regulations clarify EIC due diligence requirements and set a performance standard for the "knowledge" requirement: what a reasonable and well-informed tax return preparer, knowledgeable in the law, would do.

The "Knowledge Standard" for EIC Returns

The "knowledge standard" requires a preparer to:

- Know the law and use his knowledge of the law to ensure he is asking a client the right questions to get all relevant facts.
- Take into account what his client says and what he knows about his client.
- Not know or have reason to know any information used to determine his client's eligibility for, of the amount of, EIC is incorrect, inconsistent, or incomplete.

---

[35] The IRS uses both the terms "earned income tax credit" (EITC) and "earned income credit." They are the same credit. For consistency's sake, we will refer to it as the earned income credit, or EIC.

- Make additional inquiries if a reasonable and well-informed tax return preparer would know the information is incomplete, inconsistent, or incorrect.
- Document any additional questions he asks and his client's answers at the time of the interview.

An in-person interview is required every year with each client who is claiming the EIC.

Example: Latonya is an EA. Mai is a new client who wants to claim the EIC. She has two qualifying children. She tells Latonya she had a Schedule C business and earned $10,000 in income but had no expenses. This information appears incomplete because it is unusual that someone who is self-employed has no business expenses. Latonya is required to ask additional reasonable questions to determine if the business exists and if the information about Mai's income and expenses is correct (Publication 4687).

EIC Due Diligence and Compliance Requirements

The four due diligence requirements for preparers related to the EIC are as follows:

- **Complete and submit the Eligibility Checklist.** A preparer must complete Form 8867, *Paid Preparer's Earned Income Credit Checklist*, to make sure he considers all EIC eligibility criteria for each return prepared. He must complete the checklist based on information provided by his clients. The form must be submitted either electronically or on paper, along with any returns or claims for refund.
- **Compute the credit.** A preparer must complete the EIC worksheet in the Form 1040 series instructions or the one in Publication 596, *Earned Income Credit*. The worksheet shows what is included in the computation (i.e. self-employment income, total earned income, investment income, and adjusted gross income.) Most tax preparation software has the computation worksheet, but the IRS emphasizes that software is not a substitute for knowledge of EIC tax law.
- **Knowledge.** A preparer must not know (or have reason to know) that the information used to determine eligibility for the EIC is incorrect. A preparer must ask his client additional questions if the information furnished seems incorrect or incomplete.
- **Keeping records.** A preparer must keep a copy of Form 8867 and the EIC worksheet, as well as any additional question/answers during the client in-

terview. He also must keep copies of any documents the client gives to help determine eligibility for, or the amount of the EIC. In addition, a preparer must verify the identity of the person giving him the return information and keep a record of it. All records may be kept for at least three years in either paper or electronic format, and they must be produced if the IRS asks for them.

Example: A client states that she is separated from her spouse. Her child lives with her and she wants to claim the EIC as head of household. In reviewing the client's records it is apparent she earns a minimal income, which appears insufficient to support a household: pay rent/mortgage, utilities, food, clothing, school supplies, etc. The return preparer should ask appropriate questions to determine the client's correct filing status and determine how long the child lived with each parent during the year and probe for any additional sources of income.

Example: Judd is an EA. His new client, Thelma, 62, wants to take a dependency exemption for her son, Randy, who is 32. She also wants to claim the Earned Income Credit and the dependent care credit for her son. Since Randy is beyond the age limit for these credits, Judd makes reasonable inquiries and discovers that Randy is severely disabled and incapable of self-care. Therefore, Thelma may claim her son, and the credits will be allowed regardless of Randy's age. Judd has fulfilled his due diligence requirement by asking reasonable questions about an individual tax situation.

Paid preparers failing to meet their due diligence requirements face IRS penalties for filing incorrect EIC claims. The penalty is $500 for each failure to comply with the EIC due diligence requirements. (The penalty increased from $100 to $500 in 2011 as part of the IRS's campaign against fraudulent EIC claims.)

An employer also may be penalized for an employee's failure to exercise due diligence in the following situations:

- When an employer or principal member of management participated in or knew of the failure to comply with due diligence requirements.
- When the firm failed to establish reasonable and appropriate procedures to ensure compliance with EIC due diligence requirements.
- When the firm disregarded its compliance procedures through willfulness, recklessness, or gross indifference in the preparation of the tax return or the claim for refund.

Common EIC Errors

The IRS is always looking for abusive EIC claims. The three issues that account for more than 60 percent of all EIC errors are:

- Claiming a child who does not meet the age, relationship, or residency requirement. [36]
- Filing as single or head of household when married. [37]
- Incorrectly reporting income or expenses.

A common method of EIC fraud is the "borrowing" of dependents. Unscrupulous tax professionals will "share" one taxpayer's qualifying child or children with another taxpayer in order to allow both to claim the EIC.

Example: Reggie has four children, but he only needs the first three children to receive the maximum EIC credit. The preparer lists the first three children on the first taxpayer's return and lists the other child on another return. The preparer and Reggie are "selling" the dependents and will then split a fee or split the refund. This is an example of tax fraud, both for the preparer and the taxpayer.

Since tax professionals prepare more than 70% of EIC claims, the quality of their work has a significant impact on reducing erroneous claims. Preparers who file high percentages of questionable EIC claims or returns with a high risk of EIC error may be subject to on-site audits. IRS agents will review preparer records to verify due diligence compliance, including whether they are meeting the knowledge standard. Penalties are assessed when noncompliance is identified. The IRS focuses on reducing EIC errors by:

- Ensuring experienced preparers who filed questionable EIC claims understand the law.
- Conducting on-site due diligence audits of preparers filing returns.

---

[36] A taxpayer may claim a relative of any age as a qualifying child if the person is totally and permanently disabled and meets all other EIC requirements. The tax law definition of totally and permanently disabled is "The person cannot engage in any substantial gainful activity because of a physical or mental condition. A doctor determines the condition has lasted or the doctor expects it to last continuously for at least a year (or lead to death)."

[37] Sometimes, married couples incorrectly split their qualifying children and both file as head of household to reap the benefits of the EIC. This is considered fraudulent. IRS uses both internal information and information from external sources such as other government agencies in order to research and flag these fraudulent EIC claims.

- Barring egregious preparers with a history of noncompliance from return preparation.

EIC errors may occur for many reasons, including:

- Lack of knowledge of EIC tax law
- Honest preparer mistakes
- Intentional or unintentional client misrepresentation of facts
- Disregard for EIC due diligence requirements
- Blatant disregard of tax laws to garner erroneous refunds

Example: Esther is an EA. A new 28-year-old client wants to claim two sons, ages 14 and 15, as qualifying children for the EIC. Esther is concerned about the age of the children, since the age of the client seems inconsistent with the ages of the children claimed as sons. Esther discovers that the two boys are both adopted, which explains the age inconsistency. Esther has fulfilled her due diligence requirement and fulfilled the knowledge standard by asking probing questions to confirm the accuracy of the client's information.

Example: Jeff is single and wants to claim his daughter, Charley, for the EIC. Jeff earned $14,500 and had no other income. Charley is 35 years old and unmarried, and Jeff says she is disabled and lived with him for the full year. Charley's mother is deceased. Both Jeff and Charley have valid Social Security numbers. Charley worked for part of the year and earned $5,200. Jeff states that Charley had an accident last May and sustained a disability from the injuries. Her doctor says she is totally and permanently disabled, not able to work, and the doctor does not expect Charley to recover. Jeff can claim the EIC using Charley as his qualifying child because her doctor determined Charley cannot work because of her disability and because her disability will last longer than a year.

The IRS is attempting to educate first-time preparers whose returns reflect EIC errors. Using a scoring system to determine the degree of future risk, the agency has sent informational letters to these preparers and, in some cases, stronger compliance letters. The compliance program enforces the following:

- Outlines EIC due diligence and preparer responsibilities
- Highlights recurring errors made by other EIC return preparers to help avoid common pitfalls
- Points to tools, information, and other resources on the IRS website
- Reminds preparers that tax software is a tool, not a substitute for knowing and correctly applying the tax law

- Educates experienced preparers by mail

In February 2013, the IRS emailed tax preparers to remind them to complete the EIC checklists, saying it had received a large number of returns with incomplete information. 2012 returns with information missing on Form 8867 will be suspended, causing a potential delay in refunds.

The IRS also announced it is asking tax software companies and electronic filers to ensure that the EIC checklists are complete and remind tax preparers they could face stiff penalties without the information.[38]

Penalties for Incorrect EIC Returns

The penalties for failing to exercise due diligence with EIC claims can be severe. Incorrect EIC returns affect both the preparer and the client. If the IRS examines a client's return and denies all or part of the EIC, the client:

- Must pay back the amount in error with interest;
- May need to file Form 8862, *Information to Claim Earned Income Credit after Disallowance*;
- Cannot claim the EIC for the next two years if the IRS determines the error is because of reckless or intentional disregard of the rules; or
- Cannot claim the EIC for the next ten years if the IRS determines the error is because of fraud.

Further, if the IRS examines an EIC claim that was prepared by a tax professional and it is determined that the practitioner did not meet all four due diligence requirements, the preparer can be subject to:

- A $500 preparer penalty for each failure to comply with EIC due diligence requirements for returns required to be filed after December 31, 2011. This penalty can be assessed against an individual preparer, as well as the preparer's employer. The penalty amounts are covered in IRC Section 6695(g).
- A minimum preparer penalty of $1,000 if a practitioner prepares a client return and the IRS finds any part of the amount of taxes owed is due to an "unreasonable position."[39]

---

[38] *Accounting Today,* Feb. 4, 2013.
[39] For reference, see IRC Section 6694(a).

- A minimum preparer penalty of $5,000 if a practitioner prepares a client return and the IRS finds any part of the amount of taxes owed is due to reckless or intentional disregard of rules or regulations.[40]

If a practitioner receives a return-related penalty, he may also face:

- Disciplinary action by the OPR
- Suspension or expulsion from IRS e-file
- Injunctions barring the practitioner from preparing tax returns

The IRS has streamlined procedures for faster referrals to the U.S. Department of Justice to prohibit preparers from making fraudulent EIC claims. These preparers could be permanently or temporarily barred from any type of federal tax preparation (Publication 4687, *EITC Due Diligence*).

> **Example:** Stephanie is a return preparer working for a larger chain. She has knowingly prepared false EIC claims for several years. Eventually, the office is subject to an IRS audit, and the fraud is discovered. Stephanie is disbarred and fined. The employer is also subject to a fine under IRC § 6695(g), and can be assessed a fine for each fraudulent claim.

SSN Requirement for EIC Returns

A valid Social Security Number is required for EIC claims. If a primary taxpayer, spouse, (or both) have ITINs, they are ineligible to receive the Earned Income Tax Credit (EITC), **even if their dependents have valid SSNs**.

If a taxpayer and spouse (if filing jointly) have valid SSNs, only dependents with valid SSNs will qualify to receive EITC. In the case of a taxpayer who files a return using an ATIN (Adoption Taxpayer Identification Number), the EIC will be similarly disallowed for that dependent.

Taxpayers are allowed to amend their original returns in order to claim the EIC, if they receive valid SSNs at a later date, as long as the taxpayer otherwise qualified for the EIC at the time the original return was filed.[41]

---

[40]For reference, see IRC 6694(b)).
[41] To amend an original return to claim EIC, Form 1040X must be used.

Summary of EIC Due Diligence Requirements for Paid Preparers

Requirement	Description
1. Completion of eligibility checklist	• Make additional inquiries if a reasonable and well-informed tax return preparer would know the information is incomplete, inconsistent, or incorrect. • Document any additional questions the preparer asks and the client's answers at the time of the interview. The practitioner should also ask probing questions to determine correct eligibility.
2. Computation of the credit	• Keep the EIC worksheet that demonstrates how the EIC was computed. Preparers must complete and attach Form 8867, *Paid Preparer's Earned Income Credit Checklist*, and submit the form with all EIC refund claims. • The worksheet must show what is included in the computation: that is, self-employment income, total earned income, investment income, and adjusted gross income. Most tax software includes the computation worksheet.
3. Knowledge standard	• The preparer must know the law and use knowledge of the law to ensure he is asking the client the right questions to get all relevant facts. • He must take into account what the client says and what he knows about his client. • He must not know (or have reason to know) any information used to determine the client's eligibility for the EIC is incorrect, inconsistent, or incomplete.
4. Record Retention	• Retain Form 8867 and EIC worksheet. • Maintain records of how and when the information used to complete these forms was obtained. • Verify the identity of the person furnishing the information. • Retain all records for three years.

Unit 5: Questions

1. Which statement is correct about the EIC?

A. Information obtained by the preparer may be discarded after the tax interview.
B. Interfering with IRS efforts to investigate EIC fraud is the best thing to do.
C. Incorrectly reporting income is okay so long as the client signs a release.
D. Preparers are required to ask additional questions if the information provided by a client appears incorrect, inconsistent, or incomplete.

The answer is D. During the EIC interview with a client, preparers are required to ask additional questions if the information appears incorrect, inconsistent, or incomplete. ###

2. The IRS can impose the following ban related to the EIC:

A. The IRS cannot ban a taxpayer from claiming the EIC.
B. Ten year ban for fraud.
C. Two year ban for fraud.
D. Permanent ban for fraud.

The answer is B. The IRS can impose the following types of bans related to the EIC:
* **Two year** ban for reckless or intentional disregard of EIC rules, or
* **Ten year** ban for fraud. ###

3. What is the penalty for preparers who fail to comply with due diligence requirements for the EIC?

A. A penalty of $500 for each failure.
B. A penalty of $1,000 for each failure.
C. There is no preparer penalty, but there is a taxpayer penalty for fraud.
D. A formal reprimand by the OPR, but there is no monetary penalty.

The answer is A. Any tax return preparer who fails to comply with due diligence requirements for the EIC can be liable for a penalty of $500 for each failure. ###

4. A client tells a preparer:

•She has no Form 1099.
•She was self-employed cleaning houses.
•She earned $12,000.
•She had no expenses related to the cleaning business.

What is the BEST course of action for the preparer in this case?

A. Refuse to prepare the return based on the client's information.
B. Ask probing questions to determine the correct facts and ask for proof of income or any expenses.
C. Accept the taxpayer's word so long as she fills out a legal liability release form.
D. Make the client swear to the truthfulness of her statements before an IRS officer.

The answer is B. The best course of action would be to ask probing questions and ask for proof of income. In some cases, the client may say she had no expenses when it is not reasonable to conduct the business without incurring expenses, or the expenses may seem unreasonably high. Again, the preparer may need to ask probing questions to determine the correct facts. ###

5. When must a tax preparer complete a client checklist for the EIC?

A. Every year.
B. With every new client.
C. Every six months.
D. The client interview is recommended, but not required.

The answer is A. For any client claiming the EIC credit, a preparer must either complete Form 8867 or an equivalent checklist every single year. The preparer is required to keep a copy of the checklist in his records for three years. ###

6. All of the following are EIC due diligence requirements except:

A. To evaluate the information received from the client.
B. To apply a consistency and reasonableness standard to the information.
C. To verify the taxpayer's information with the appropriate third parties.
D. To make additional reasonable inquiries when the information appears to be incorrect, inconsistent, or incomplete.

The answer is C. A tax professional is not required to verify a taxpayer's answers with third parties. The EIC due diligence requires a paid preparer to:
- Evaluate the information received from the client,
- Apply a consistency and reasonableness standard to the information,
- Make additional reasonable inquiries when the information appears to be incorrect, inconsistent, or incomplete, and
- Document additional inquiries and the client's response. ###

7. All of the following are common errors taxpayers make in claiming the EIC except:

A. Incorrectly reporting income or expenses.
B. Incorrectly claiming a child who does not meet the specific EIC requirements.
C. Filing as head of household when married.
D. Listing earned income for the year.

The answer is D. To qualify for the EIC, a taxpayer must have earned income during the tax period. Assuming it is reported correctly, listing earned income is not a common error made in claiming the EIC. The IRS cites the other three errors as common issues it sees with EIC claims. ###

8. All of the following are possible penalties for preparers who file fraudulent EIC claims except:

A. Suspension or expulsion from IRS e-file.
B. Criminal action undertaken by the OPR.
C. A ban from preparing tax returns.
D. A preparer penalty of $5,000 if the IRS finds any part of the amount of taxes owed is due to reckless or intentional disregard of rules or regulations.

The answer is B. The OPR may initiate disciplinary actions against preparers who violate rules related to the EIC. However, the OPR never initiates or prosecutes *criminal* cases. ###

9. Which is not one of the four due diligence requirements preparers are expected to follow for EIC claims?

A. Maintaining records for two years.
B. Completing the eligibility checklist.
C. Computation of the credit.
D. The knowledge standard.

The answer is A. Under the record retention portion of the due diligence requirements, records must be maintained for three years, not two. ###

10. Mack and Judy have valid ITINs. They have two children, both of whom have valid SSNs. Assuming they meet the income requirements, can Mack and Judy claim EIC?

A. They may claim the EIC for themselves and their children
B. They can claim EIC for their children, but not for themselves
C. They cannot claim EIC, regardless of whether their children have valid SSNs
D. Their dependents can claim EIC, but only if they file separate returns

The answer is C. If a primary taxpayer, spouse, (or both) have ITINs, they are ineligible to receive the Earned Income Tax Credit (EITC), even if their dependents have valid SSNs. ###

Unit 6: Covered Opinions

      The Circular 230 requirements apply to all written forms of federal tax advice. There are especially strict rules for the written advice on "covered opinions," which are sometimes referred to as "tax shelter advice." The rules are extremely complex, and are in the process of being revised.[42]

      Firms are required to have procedures in place to ensure compliance with the IRS regulations on covered opinions. Tax shelters themselves are not prohibited; some are fine. A pretax retirement plan, for example, is considered a legal tax shelter. However, some tax shelters are unlawful.

Covered Opinions (Tax Shelter Opinions)

      Covered opinions relate to the advice a practitioner gives a client regarding a tax shelter. IRS regulations provide mandatory requirements for practitioners who provide covered opinions, which are defined as follows:

- Any transaction the IRS has determined is a tax-avoidance transaction.
- Any plan or arrangement that has tax avoidance as a principal purpose.
- Any plan or arrangement that has tax avoidance as a principal purpose if the written advice is either:
    - A reliance opinion
    - A marketed opinion
    - Subject to the conditions of confidentiality
    - Subject to contractual protection[43]

Reliance opinion: Written advice that is more likely than not (greater than 50%) of being sustained in the taxpayer's favor.

Marketed opinion: Written advice that is used by another person other than the practitioner in promoting, marketing, or recommending an investment plan to one or more taxpayers.

---

[42] In September 2012, the IRS submitted proposed revisions to Section 10.35 of Circular 230. The revisions would revoke the complicated rules regarding covered opinions and substitute them with a single, basic new standard governing all written tax advice. As of publication, these new rules have not yet become final; thus exam-takers should study the current rules of Circular 230 covered in this unit.
[43] Circular §230(b)(2)(C), §230(C)(4)(i) and §230(C)(5)(I)

Under the rules, unless the advice contains a disclaimer,[44] the practitioner providing advice about a covered opinion must comply with ALL of the following requirements:

- The practitioner must use due diligence in fact finding.
- All pertinent facts must be separately stated and disclosed, and not be deemed unreasonable or immaterial by the practitioner.
- The opinion must relate the facts to applicable law standards without inconsistency.
- All significant federal tax issues must be addressed and disclosed in the written advice.

The practitioner has a duty to also consider the impact of federal tax issues and provide a conclusion about whether the taxpayer's position on each issue is likely to prevail.

Requirements for Covered Opinions

General standards for practitioners who offer covered opinions are set forth in §10.35. Practitioners who provide covered opinions are required to:

1. **Know all the relevant facts:** A practitioner must describe a legitimate business purpose for the transaction, and he must use reasonable efforts to get the factual information correct.
2. **Relate law to the facts:** The opinion must relate law to the facts.
3. **Evaluation of significant tax issues:** The opinion must provide that the taxpayer will prevail (more likely than not) on the merit of the issues contained in the opinion.
4. **Overall conclusion:** The practitioner must provide an overall conclusion that the tax treatment is proper and give reasons for that conclusion.
5. **Practitioner competence:** The practitioner must be competent and knowledgeable about the issues addressed in the opinion.

When practitioners put tax shelter advice in writing, the following is expected under §10.37:

---

[44] In practical fact, many practitioners now routinely add a disclaimer to any written communication, including e-mails, regardless of whether the communication contains tax advice. According to the IRS, this practice may actually discourage compliance with ethical requirements because some practitioners believe a disclaimer allows them to disregard the current Section 10.35 standards governing written tax advice. This issue is one of the factors behind the IRS's proposal to overhaul the covered opinion regulations.

- A practitioner must not make *unreasonable* factual or legal assumptions.
- A practitioner must not have an *unreasonable reliance* on taxpayer information or third party information.
- The practitioner must consider all relevant facts and law.
- The possibility of an IRS audit cannot be a factor.

Excluded Advice (Not Considered Covered Opinions)

Some forms of written tax advice are not subject to the strict rules for covered opinions under Circular 230. Certain types of "excluded advice" that do not qualify as covered opinions include:

- Advice from in-house employees to their employers.
- Written advice solely for one taxpayer after the taxpayer has already filed a tax return.
- Written advice that does not resolve a federal tax issue in the taxpayer's favor. This is also called "negative advice," wherein an advisor tells a client a transaction will not provide the purported tax benefit.
- Written advice regarding qualified plans, state and local bonds, or SEC-filed documents.
- Any written advice if the practitioner is reasonably expected to provide subsequent written advice that satisfies the covered opinion requirements.

Example: An accountant is working full-time as an employee for Baker's Dozen Corporation. The accountant gives incorrect advice to his employer regarding a tax shelter, and the employer is subject to penalties. The employee is not subject to Circular 230 penalties for covered opinions because he was acting as an in-house professional for his own employer.

Written advice will not be treated as a "reliance opinion" if the practitioner openly discloses that it was not intended to be used by the taxpayer to avoid penalties.

Reporting Requirements for Tax Shelter Activities

There are special types of tax shelter activities that must be reported to the IRS. If a taxpayer participates in any activity that the IRS has deemed to be a "tax avoidance" activity and a tax shelter, the activity must be disclosed on the taxpayer's return. Form 8886, *Reportable Transaction Disclosure Statement*, must be attached to a taxpayer's return for any year that he participates in a tax shelter.

Any taxpayer (individual or business) that participates in a reportable transaction must file Form 8886. Tax advisors also must disclose the transaction to the IRS. In addition, the tax practitioner is required to maintain a list of investors that must be furnished to the IRS upon request. Substantial penalties apply both to taxpayers and material advisors for noncompliance on either issue.

The fact that a tax shelter transaction must be reported on this form does not mean the tax benefits from such a transaction will be disallowed by the IRS. A taxpayer may also request a ruling from the IRS to determine whether a transaction must be disclosed.

A person who sells (or otherwise transfers) an interest in a tax shelter must provide the taxpayer the tax shelter registration number or be subject to a $100 penalty.

If a taxpayer claims any deduction, credit, or other tax benefit because of a tax shelter, he must attach Form 8271, *Investor Reporting of Tax Shelter Registration Number*, to the tax return to report this number. A taxpayer may have to pay a penalty of $250 for each failure to report a tax shelter registration number on a return.

Standards for Tax Returns and Documents §10.34

A practitioner may not willfully sign a tax return or claim for refund that the practitioner knows (or reasonably should know) contains a position that:

- Is frivolous
- Lacks a reasonable basis
- Is an unreasonable position as described in Section 6694(a)(2) of the Internal Revenue Code[45]
- Is a willful attempt by the practitioner to understate the liability for tax or a reckless or intentional disregard of rules or regulations

A tax professional cannot knowingly sign a frivolous return. A frivolous position is defined as one that the preparer knows is in bad faith and is improper.

The IRS will take into account a pattern of conduct in determining whether a practitioner acted willfully, recklessly, or through gross incompetence.

---

[45] Section 6694(a) imposes penalties on paid practitioners who prepare returns reflecting an understatement of liability due to an "unreasonable position" if the practitioner knew (or reasonably should have known) of the position. No penalty is imposed, however, if it is shown that there is reasonable cause for the understatement and the tax return preparer acted in good faith.

A practitioner may not advise a client to submit a document, affidavit, or other paper to the IRS:

- The purpose of which is to delay or impede the administration of the federal tax laws;
- That is frivolous; or
- That contains or omits information in a manner that demonstrates an intentional disregard of a rule or regulation unless the practitioner also advises the client to submit a document that evidences a good faith challenge to the rule or regulation (such as a disclosure statement).

A practitioner must make a reasonable attempt to determine if the taxpayer's position, especially a tax shelter position, will be sustained on its merits.

Advising Clients on Potential Penalties

A practitioner is required to inform a client of any penalties that are reasonably likely to apply to a position taken on a tax return if:

- The practitioner advised the client with respect to the position; or
- The practitioner prepared or signed the tax return.

The practitioner also must inform the client of any opportunity to avoid penalties by disclosure and of the requirements for adequate disclosure. This rule applies even if the practitioner is not subject to a penalty under the Internal Revenue Code related to the position or to the document or tax return submitted.

A position is considered to have a realistic possibility of being sustained on its merits "if a reasonable and well-informed analysis by a person knowledgeable in the tax law would lead such a person to conclude that the position has a greater likelihood of being sustained on its merits."

A practitioner may still sign a return containing a position that does not meet the "more likely than not" standard so long as the position has a reasonable basis, is not frivolous, and is adequately disclosed. Positions taken by tax professionals on returns must meet certain standards. A position must meet at least ONE of these two standards:

- The position is "more likely than not" to be sustained on its merits, OR
- The position must have a "reasonable basis."

Example: Amanda is an EA with a client who has a very complex tax situation. She notices that the IRS publications reflect one position, but there is a recent court case that may allow a more favorable position for her client. There are also two other similar cases being litigated, but the outcome of those cases is currently unknown. Amanda believes that the position has a 20% chance of prevailing on its merits. Amanda thinks that the client's position has a "reasonable basis" and decides to disclose the position on the tax return. Even though the position is contrary to the IRS' current guidance, Amanda may take the position on the return, as long as it is disclosed. She should file Form 8275 along with the tax return stating the position, referencing the court case or any other basis she has for the position.

Definitions:

- **More likely than not:** There is a *greater than* 50% likelihood that the tax treatment will be upheld if the IRS challenges it. If a preparer is unsure that a position meets this standard, he may still avoid penalties by disclosing the position on the return. However, a disclosure statement will not protect the preparer if the position is patently frivolous.[46]

- **Reasonable basis:** A position is considered to have a reasonable basis if it is reasonably based on one or more of the authorities of the substantial understatement penalty regulations. "Reasonable basis" is a relatively high standard of tax reporting that is significantly higher than "not frivolous." The "reasonable basis" standard is not satisfied by a return position that is merely arguable. Under the "reasonable basis" standard, a preparer is required to inform the taxpayer of the penalties that may be assessed on the client under Section 6662.

Disclosure Statements

A practitioner must inform a client of the penalties reasonably likely to apply, of any opportunity to avoid any penalty by disclosure, and of the requirements for adequate disclosure. In the case of a tax return that requires a disclosure, the position should be disclosed to the IRS on either Form 8275, *Disclosure Statement*, or Form 8275-R, *Regulation Disclosure Statement*.

Form 8275 is used by taxpayers and preparers to disclose positions that are not otherwise adequately disclosed on a tax return to avoid certain penalties. It can

---

[46] See Regulation 1.6694-1(e) for more information.

also be used for disclosures relating to preparer penalties for understatements due to unreasonable positions or disregard of rules.

The disclosure can be used to avoid accuracy-related penalties so long as the return position has a reasonable basis (such as a recent court case in the taxpayer's favor). The penalty will not be imposed if there was reasonable cause for the position and the taxpayer (and preparer) acted in good faith in taking the position.

As detailed earlier in Unit 4, if there is an understatement on a tax return due to an unrealistic position, the preparer penalty is the greater of:

- $1,000 per tax return, or

- 50% of the additional income upon which the penalty was imposed.

This applies when a preparer knows, or reasonably should have known, that the position was unrealistic and would not have been sustained on its merits.

If a taxpayer files a frivolous income tax return, a penalty of $5,000 can be assessed under Section 6702. There are also penalties that can be imposed on preparers who file frivolous returns. The penalty for a frivolous position in the U.S. Tax Court is $25,000.

The "reasonable basis" rule does not apply to tax shelters. That is because a tax shelter must always be disclosed, regardless of any possibility standard.

Reportable Transactions

A "reportable transaction" is a transaction that the IRS has determined as having a potential for tax avoidance or tax evasion. If a reportable transaction is not disclosed and results in an understatement of tax, an additional penalty in the amount of 30 percent of the understatement may be assessed. Reportable transactions must be reported on **Form 8886,** *Reportable Transaction Disclosure Statement.*

A separate statement must be filed for each reportable transaction. The following losses are not considered "reportable transactions:"

- Losses from casualties, thefts, and condemnations
- Losses from Ponzi Schemes
- Losses from the sale or exchange of an asset with a qualifying basis
- Losses arising from any mark-to-market treatment of an item

Reportable transactions are also called "listed transactions." The rules for reportable transactions apply to all entities and individuals, (including trusts, estates, partnerships, S corporations, etc). Any of these entities that participates in a reportable transaction is required to file Form 8886.

Unit 6: Questions

1. Which of the following types of written advice would fall under the Circular 230 rules for "covered opinions"?

A. Advice from in-house employees to their employers.
B. Written advice solely for one taxpayer after the taxpayer has already filed a tax return.
C. Written advice that does not resolve a federal tax issue in the taxpayer's favor.
D. A plan or arrangement whose principal purpose is the avoidance of tax.

The answer is D. The rules regarding "covered opinions" include the written advice regarding a plan or arrangement whose principal purpose is the avoidance or evasion of any tax. ###

2. A tax professional cannot knowingly sign _____.

A. A tax return for a family member.
B. A tax return that is not prepared for compensation.
C. A tax return with a properly disclosed tax shelter position.
D. A frivolous return with a disclosure.

The answer is D. A tax professional cannot sign a frivolous return, even if the return has a disclosure. A frivolous position is defined as one that the preparer knows is in bad faith and is improper. ###

3. Reportable transactions are also called _____.
A. Listed transactions.
B. Loss transactions.
C. Tax transactions.
D. Government transactions.

The answer is A. Reportable transactions are also called "listed transactions."

4. Dylan is a client of Bethany's, an EA. Dylan wishes to claim a deduction for a large business expense. However, there is a question about whether the expense is "ordinary and necessary" for his business. If the deduction were disallowed, there would be a substantial understatement of tax (over 25%). Bethany researches the issue and tells Dylan that the position should be disclosed. Dylan doesn't want to disclose the position on the return, because he is afraid that the IRS will disallow it. What are the repercussions for Bethany?

A. None. All the penalties apply to the client.
B. Bethany may be liable for preparer penalties.
C. Bethany will not be liable for preparer penalties so long as she explains the potential penalties to the client.
D. None of the above.

The answer is B. If Bethany does not adequately disclose the position and the return is later examined by the IRS, she may be subject to a preparer penalty. The disclosure form is filed to avoid the portions of the accuracy-related penalty due to disregard of rules or to a substantial understatement of income tax. ###

5. What is the penalty for failure to furnish a tax shelter registration number on a return?

A. $150 for each failure.
B. $250 for each failure.
C. $500 for each failure.
D. $1,000 for each failure.

The answer is B. A taxpayer may have to pay a penalty of $250 for each failure to report a tax shelter registration number on a return. ###

6. A practitioner is required to inform a client of any penalties that are reasonably likely to apply to a position taken on a tax return if:

A. The taxpayer decides to self-prepare a return.
B. The practitioner gave the client professional advice on the position.
C. The IRS has the taxpayer under examination.
D. The taxpayer is deceased.

The answer is B. A practitioner is required to inform a client of any penalties that are reasonably likely to apply to a position taken on a tax return if:
- The practitioner advised the client with respect to the position; or
- The practitioner prepared or signed the tax return. ###

7. When it comes to professional tax advice, the IRS defines "more likely than not" as:

A. A tax treatment that has a reasonable basis and at least a 10% likelihood of being upheld in court.
B. A tax treatment that has at least a 50% likelihood that the position will be upheld if the IRS challenges it.
C. A tax treatment that has a greater than 50% likelihood that the position will be upheld if the IRS challenges it.
D. A tax treatment that is disclosed.

The answer is C. The IRS defines "more likely than not" as a position that has a greater than 50% likelihood that the tax treatment will be upheld if the IRS challenges it. A position is considered to have a realistic possibility of being sustained on its merits "if a reasonable and well-informed analysis by a person knowledgeable in the tax law would lead such a person to conclude that the position has a greater likelihood of being sustained on its merits." ###

8. A "marketed opinion" is defined as:

A. Written advice concerning tax shelters.
B. An opinion that has a more than likelihood (greater than 50%) of being sustained in the taxpayer's favor.
C. A form of due diligence related to marketing a preparer's tax practice.
D. An opinion that is used by another person other than the practitioner in promoting, marketing, or recommending an investment plan to one or more taxpayers.

The answer is D. A marketed opinion is included under the guidelines of Section 10.35. It is an opinion that is used by another person other than the practitioner in promoting, marketing, or recommending an investment plan to one or more taxpayers. Answer "B" defines a "reliance opinion," which is also included in the covered opinion regulations. ###

Unit 7: The IRS Collection Process

More Reading:
Publication 594, *The Collection Process*
Publication 1035, *Extending the Tax Assessment Period*
Publication 971, *Innocent Spouse Relief*
Publication 556, *Examination of Returns, Appeal Rights, and Claims for Refund*
Publication 1660, *Collection Appeal Rights*

The IRS has wide powers when it comes to collecting unpaid taxes. If a taxpayer does not pay in full when filing his tax return, he will receive a bill from an IRS service center. The first notice will be a letter that explains the balance due and demands payment in full. It will include the amount of the tax plus any penalties and interest added to the taxpayer's unpaid balance from the date the tax was due.

This first notice starts the collection process, which continues until the taxpayer's account is satisfied or until the IRS may no longer legally collect the tax, such as when the collection period has expired.

The IRS has **ten years** from the date of assessment to collect a tax debt from a taxpayer. If a taxpayer does not file a tax return, the statute of limitations does not expire.

The statute of limitations on collection can also be suspended by various acts. The ten-year collection period is *suspended* in the following cases:

- While the IRS and the Office of Appeals consider a request for an installment agreement or an offer in compromise
- From the date a taxpayer requests a collection due process (CDP) hearing
- While the taxpayer is residing outside the United States
- For tax periods included in a bankruptcy

The amount of time the suspension is in effect will be added to the time remaining in the ten-year period. For example, if the ten-year period is suspended for six months, the time left in the period the IRS has to collect will increase by six months.

The IRS is required to notify the taxpayer that he may refuse to extend the statute of limitations.

Filing a petition in bankruptcy automatically stays assessment and collection of tax. The stay remains in effect until the bankruptcy court discharges liabilities or lifts the stay.

Statute of Limitations for Collection and Refunds	
Claim for refund	Three years from the date the original return was filed or the return was due (whichever is later), or two years from the date the tax was paid, whichever is later.
IRS assessment	Three years after the due date of the return, or three years after the date the return was actually filed, which-ever is later. There are exceptions for outright fraud, fail-ure-to-file, extension by agreement, and substantial omission (over 25% of income).
Collection action	Ten years from the date of a tax assessment.

Actions the IRS Uses to Collect Unpaid Taxes

If taxes are not paid timely, the law requires that enforcement action be taken, which may include the following:

- Issuing a notice of levy on salary and other income, bank accounts, or property (legally seizing property to satisfy the tax debt).
- Assessing a trust fund recovery penalty for unpaid employment taxes.
- Issuing a summons to secure information to prepare unfiled tax returns or determine the taxpayer's ability to pay. IRS employees will prepare "substitute returns"[47] when taxpayers do not file voluntarily.
- Filing a notice of a federal tax lien.
- Offsetting a taxpayer's refund.

In addition, the IRS will apply future federal tax refunds to any prior amount due. Any state income tax refunds may also be applied to a taxpayer's federal tax liability.

---

[47] These substitute returns generally do not give credit for deductions and exemptions a taxpayer may be entitled to receive. Even if the IRS has already filed a substitute return, a taxpayer may still file his own return. The IRS will generally adjust the taxpayer's account to reflect the correct figures.

Federal Tax Lien

The federal tax lien is a claim against a taxpayer's property, including property that the taxpayer acquires even after the lien is filed. By filing a notice of federal tax lien, the IRS establishes its interest in the property as a creditor. Liens give the IRS a legal claim to a taxpayer's property as security for his tax debt. A notice of federal tax lien may be filed only after:

- The IRS assesses the taxpayer's liability;
- The IRS sends a notice and demand for payment; and
- The taxpayer neglects to pay the debt.

Once these requirements are met, a lien is created for the amount of the taxpayer's debt. By filing notice of this lien, the taxpayer's creditors are publicly notified that the IRS has a claim against all the taxpayer's property, including property acquired *after* the lien is filed. The lien attaches to all the taxpayer's property (such as a house or car) and to all the taxpayer's "rights" to property (such as accounts receivable, in the case of a business).

Once a lien is filed, the IRS generally cannot release the lien[48] until the taxes are paid in full or until the IRS may no longer legally collect the tax (the statute of limitations runs out).

Notice of Levy and IRS Seizures

The IRS will send a notice of levy to a taxpayer before it confiscates his property. A levy allows the IRS to confiscate and sell property to satisfy a tax debt. This property could include a car, boat, or real estate.

The IRS may also levy wages, bank accounts, Social Security benefits, and retirement income. The IRS may also apply future federal tax refunds to prior year tax debt, or state income tax refunds may be routed to the IRS an applied to a tax liability.

An IRS levy refers to the actual *seizing of property* authorized by an earlier filed tax lien. If a tax lien is the IRS's authorization to act by seizing property, then the IRS levy is the actual act of seizure. The following items are exempt from IRS levy:

- Wearing apparel and school books.

---

[48]See Publication 1450, *Request for Release of Federal Tax Lien*, for more information.

- Fuel, provisions (food), furniture, personal effects in the taxpayer's household, arms for personal use, or livestock, up to $8,570 in value for tax year 2012.
- Books and tools necessary for the trade, business, or profession of the taxpayer, up to $4,290 in value for tax year 2012.
- Undelivered mail.
- Unemployment benefits and amounts payable under the Job Training Partnership Act.
- Workers' compensation, including amounts payable to dependents.
- Certain annuity or pension payments, but only if payable by the Army, Navy, Air Force, Coast Guard, or under the Railroad Retirement Act or Railroad Unemployment Insurance Act. Traditional or Roth IRAs are not exempt from levy.
- Judgments for the support of minor children (child support).
- Certain public assistance and welfare payments, and amounts payable for Supplemental Security Income for the aged, blind, and disabled under the Social Security Act. Regular Social Security payments are not exempt from levy.

If an IRS levy is creating an immediate economic hardship, it may be released. A levy release does not mean the taxpayer is exempt from paying the balance.

IRS Seizures

An IRS seizure is the legal act of confiscating a taxpayer's property to satisfy a tax debt. There are special rules regarding IRS seizures. The IRS must wait at least 30 days from the date the notice of intent to seize is given before it can make a seizure. Typically, the IRS may not seize property in the following circumstances:

- When there is a pending installment agreement
- While a taxpayer's appeal is pending
- During the consideration of an offer in compromise
- During a bankruptcy (unless the seizure is *authorized* by the bankruptcy court)
- If the taxpayer's liability is $5,000 or less in a seizure of real property (real estate)
- While innocent spouse claims are pending

The IRS may not seize a principal residence without prior approval from the IRS district director or assistant district director. Judicial approval is required for most principal residence seizures. The IRS may still seize or levy property if the collection of tax is in jeopardy.

Collection Appeal Rights

A taxpayer may appeal IRS collection actions to the IRS Office of Appeals. The Office of Appeals is separate from and independent of the IRS Collection office that initiated the collection action.

The IRS ensures the independence of the Appeals office by adhering to a strict policy of no *ex parte* communication[49] with the IRS Collection office about the accuracy of the facts or the merits of each case without providing the taxpayer an opportunity to participate at that meeting.

The two main procedures are "collection due process" and the "collection appeals program."

Collection Due Process Hearings (CDP)

A taxpayer who receives a notice may request a collection due process (CDP) hearing by completing Form 12153, *Request for a Collection Due Process or Equivalent Hearing,* and submitting it to the address listed on the IRS notice. Collection due process is available for the following notices:

- Notice of federal tax lien filing
- Final notice: notice of intent to levy
- Notice of jeopardy levy and right of appeal
- Notice of levy on a state tax refund
- Notice of levy with respect to a disqualified employment tax levy

After a taxpayer receives one of these notices, he has 30 days to file a request for a CDP hearing protesting the IRS's collection action. The taxpayer (or his representative) will then meet with an Appeals officer.

---

[49]An "ex parte communication" occurs when a party to a case communicates directly with another party about issues in the case without the other party's knowledge. In this case, the IRS Collection office is prohibited from direct communication with the Appeals office. This allows the Appeals office to function independently of the collection arm of the IRS. Revenue Procedure 2000-43 has more information about Appeals' mandatory independence and ex parte communication, and is available at *www.IRS.gov.*

Many taxpayers will ignore IRS notices until they receive a final notice or a notice of intent to levy. Often, by the time this happens, it is too late to help the taxpayer solve these issues, and the IRS has already begun the collection process in earnest.

Some of the issues that may be discussed during a collection due process hearing include:

- Whether or not the taxpayer paid all the tax owed
- If the IRS assessed tax and sent the levy notice when the taxpayer was in bankruptcy
- Whether the IRS made a procedural error in the assessment
- Whether the time to collect the tax (the statute of limitations) has expired
- If the taxpayer wishes to discuss collection options
- If the taxpayer wishes to make a spousal defense (innocent spouse relief)

After the hearing, the Appeals officer will issue a written determination letter.

If the taxpayer disagrees with the Appeals officer's determination, he can appeal to the U.S. Tax Court (or other court). No collection action can be taken against the taxpayer while the determination of the Appeals officer is being challenged in Tax Court.

Collection Appeals Program (CAP)

The collection appeals program (CAP) is generally quicker than a CDP hearing and available for a broader range of collection actions. However, the taxpayer cannot go to court to appeal if he disagrees with a CAP decision. CAP is available for the following actions:

- Before or after the IRS files a notice of federal tax lien
- Before or after the IRS levies or seizes the taxpayer's property
- After the termination of an installment agreement
- After the rejection of an installment agreement

A taxpayer may represent himself, or the taxpayer may choose to appoint a qualified representative (attorney, CPA, EA, or spouse or family member). In the case of a business, the entity may be represented by regular full-time employees, general partners, or bona fide officers.

Taxpayer Advocate Service

The Taxpayer Advocate Service (TAS) is an independent organization within the IRS whose goal is to help taxpayers resolve problems with the IRS. A taxpayer may be eligible for TAS assistance when he is facing the following situations:

- Economic harm or significant cost (including fees for professional representation)
- A significant delay to resolve a tax issue
- No response or resolution to a problem by the date promised by the IRS
- Irreparable injury or long-term adverse impact if relief is not granted

The Taxpayer Advocate Service is free and confidential, and is available for businesses as well as individuals.

Example: Geraldine filed an amended return for 2012 over three months ago. She has an outstanding balance for the prior tax year and has been receiving IRS collection notices. Geraldine's expected refund would fully pay her balance due and leave her with a small refund. The official processing time for Form 1040X, *Amended U.S. Individual Income Tax Return*, is approximately eight to twelve weeks. However, she has been waiting more than three months for her refund to process. She has contacted the IRS numerous times about the delay, but was never given a reason for the delay. Geraldine may request intervention from the TAS.

Seeking Relief from Joint Liability

Many married taxpayers choose to file jointly because of certain benefits this filing status allows. In the case of a joint return, both taxpayers are liable for the tax and any interest or penalty even if they later separate or divorce.

"Joint and several liability" means that each taxpayer is legally responsible for the entire liability. Thus, both spouses are generally held responsible for all the tax due even if only one spouse earned all the income. This is true even if the divorce decree states that a former spouse will be responsible for any amounts due on previously filed joint returns.

In some cases, however, a spouse can get relief from joint liability. There are three types of relief from joint and several liability [50] for spouses who filed joint returns:

1. **Innocent Spouse Relief:** Provides relief from additional tax if a spouse or former spouse failed to report income or claimed improper deductions.

2. **Separation of Liability Relief:** Provides for the allocation of additional tax owed between the taxpayer and his spouse or former spouse because an item was not reported properly on a joint return. The tax allocated to the taxpayer is the amount for which he is responsible.

3. **Equitable Relief:** May apply when a taxpayer does not qualify for innocent spouse relief or separation of liability relief for something not reported properly on a joint return and generally attributable to the taxpayer's spouse. A taxpayer may also qualify for equitable relief if the correct amount of tax was reported on his joint return but the tax remains unpaid.

Requesting Innocent Spouse Relief

The taxpayer must meet ALL of the following conditions in order to qualify for innocent spouse relief:

- The taxpayer filed a joint return, which has an understatement of tax, directly related to his spouse's erroneous items.
- The taxpayer establishes that at the time he signed the joint return he did not know and had no reason to know that there was an understatement of tax.
- Taking into account all the facts and circumstances, it would be unfair for the IRS to hold the taxpayer liable for the understatement.

In order to apply for innocent spouse relief, a taxpayer must submit Form 8857, *Request for Innocent Spouse Relief,* and sign it under penalty of perjury.

A request for innocent spouse relief will be denied if the IRS proves that the taxpayer and spouse or former spouse transferred property to one another as part

---

[50]**Joint And Several Liability:** This is when multiple parties can be held liable for the same act and be responsible for all restitution. For the IRS, this means that on a joint return, both spouses will typically be responsible for the tax, even if only one spouse has income or is responsible for the tax. One way for a taxpayer to avoid joint and several liability is to file for innocent spouse relief.

of a fraudulent scheme to defraud the IRS or another third party, such as a creditor, ex-spouse, or business partner.

If a taxpayer requests innocent spouse relief, the IRS cannot enforce collection action while the request is pending. But interest and penalties continue to accrue.

> **Example:** Nancy and Allen are married and file jointly. At the time Nancy signed their joint return, she was unaware that her husband had a gambling problem. The IRS examined their joint return several months later and determined that Allen's unreported gambling winnings were $25,000. Nancy was able to prove that she did not know about, and had no reason to know about, the additional $25,000 because of the way her spouse concealed his gambling winnings. The understatement of tax due to the $25,000 qualifies for innocent spouse relief.

Requesting Separation of Liability Relief

To qualify for separation of liability relief, the taxpayer must have filed a joint return. Separation of liability applies to taxpayers who are:

(1) No longer married, or
(2) Legally separated, or
(3) Living apart for the 12 months prior to the filing of a claim. (A taxpayer also qualifies if he or she is widowed.)

"Living apart" does not include a spouse who is only temporarily absent from the household. A temporary absence exists if it is reasonable to assume the absent spouse will return to the household, or a substantially equivalent household is maintained in anticipation of such a return. A temporary absence may be due to imprisonment, illness, business, vacation, military service, or education. In this case, the taxpayer would not qualify for separation of liability relief.

The spouse or former spouse who is applying for separation of liability relief must not have known about the understatement of tax at the time of signing the return. An exception is made for spousal abuse or domestic violence, if the taxpayer had been afraid that failing to sign the return could result in harm or retaliation.

Requesting Equitable Relief

A taxpayer may still qualify for equitable relief if he does not qualify for innocent spouse relief or separation of liability relief. Equitable relief is available for additional tax owed because of:

- A reporting error (an understatement), or
- When a taxpayer has properly reported the tax but was unable to pay the tax due (an underpayment).

To qualify for equitable relief, the taxpayer must establish, under all the facts and circumstances, that it would be unfair to hold him liable for the understatement or underpayment of tax. The IRS also considers a taxpayer's current marital status, whether there is a legal obligation under a divorce decree to pay the tax, and whether he or she would suffer significant economic hardship if relief were not granted. According to the IRS, the following factors weigh in favor of equitable relief:

- Abuse by the spouse or former spouse
- Poor mental or physical health on the date the taxpayer signed the return or requested relief

This is a major shift in policy concerning equitable relief, which the IRS used to grant only in rare circumstances. Under new guidelines, the agency says it will be more likely to grant equitable relief when one spouse has abused the other or exerted "financial control" over money matters.

The agency also is no longer enforcing a two-year time limit for filing equitable relief claims, which is expected to greatly increase the number of claims granted. Starting in 2011, spousal requests for equitable relief are no longer required to be submitted within two years of IRS collection activity. Under this new provision, many taxpayers may even qualify for retroactive relief.

A taxpayer whose equitable relief request was previously denied solely due to the two-year limit, may reapply using IRS Form 8857, *Request for Innocent Spouse Relief,* as long as the collection statute of limitations for the tax years involved has not expired.

The IRS will not apply the two-year limit in any pending litigation involving equitable relief, and where litigation is final, the IRS will suspend collection action under certain circumstances.[51]

> **Example:** Paula and Joshua were married in 2011 and filed a joint return that showed they owed $10,000. Paula had $5,000 of her own money and she took out a loan to pay the other $5,000. Paula gave Joshua the money to pay the $10,000 liability. Without telling Paula, Joshua spent $5,000 on himself. The couple was divorced in 2012. Paula had no knowledge at the time she signed the return that the tax would not be paid. These facts indicate to the IRS that it may be unfair to hold Paula liable for the $5,000 underpayment. The IRS will consider these facts, together with all the other facts and circumstances, to determine whether to grant Paula equitable relief from the $5,000 underpayment.

Injured Spouse Claims

"Innocent spouse relief" should not be confused with an "injured spouse" claim. These are completely different claims. A taxpayer may qualify as an injured spouse if he files a joint return and his share of the refund was applied against past due amounts owed by a spouse.

An injured spouse may be entitled to recoup only **his share** of a tax refund. In this way, injured spouse relief differs from innocent spouse relief. When a joint return is filed and the refund is used to pay one spouse's past-due federal tax, state income tax, child support, spousal support, or federal nontax debt (such as a delinquent student loan), the other spouse may be considered an injured spouse. The injured spouse can get back his share of the refund using Form 8379, *Injured Spouse Allocation*.

> **Example:** Trudy and Brent marry in 2011 and file jointly in 2012. Unbeknownst to Trudy, Brent has outstanding unpaid child support and old delinquent student loan debt. Their entire refund is retained in order to pay Brent's outstanding debt and back child support. In this case, Trudy may qualify for injured spouse treatment. This means that she may be able to recoup *her share* of the tax refund. Brent's share of the refund will be retained by the IRS to pay the delinquent debt.

---

[51] For more information, see IRS Publication 971, *Innocent Spouse Relief.*

IRS Offer in Compromise Program

An offer in compromise (OIC) is an agreement between a taxpayer and the IRS that settles the taxpayer's tax liabilities for less than the full amount owed. Absent special circumstances, an offer will not be accepted if the IRS believes that the liability can be paid in full as a lump sum or through a payment agreement.

An offer in compromise can be applied to all taxes, including interest and penalties. A taxpayer may submit an OIC on three grounds:

Doubt as to Collectability

Doubt exists that the taxpayer could ever pay the full amount of tax liability owed within the remainder of the statutory period for collection.

Example: Elise owes $80,000 for unpaid tax liabilities and agrees that the tax she owes is correct. Elise is terminally ill, cannot work, and is on disability. She does not own any real property and does not have the ability to fully pay the liability now or through monthly installment payments.

Doubt as to Liability

A legitimate doubt exists that the assessed tax liability is correct.

*Note: If a taxpayer submits an OIC under "doubt as to liability," **no payment** is required with the submission.

Example: Sofia was vice president of a corporation from 2005 to 2011. In 2012, the corporation accrued unpaid payroll taxes and Sofia was assessed a trust fund recovery penalty. However, by 2012, Sofia had resigned from the corporation and was no longer a corporate officer. Since she had resigned prior to the payroll taxes accruing and was not contacted prior to the assessment, there is legitimate doubt that the assessed tax liability is correct. She may apply for an OIC under "doubt as to liability."

> ## Effective Tax Administration
>
> There is no doubt that the tax is correct and there is potential to collect the full amount of the tax owed, but an exceptional circumstance exists that would allow the IRS to consider an OIC. To be eligible for compromise on this basis, a taxpayer must demonstrate that the collection of the tax would create serious economic hardship or would be unfair and inequitable. It is extremely rare for the IRS to approve an OIC on these grounds.
>
> **Example:** Brad and Stacy Snyder are married and have assets sufficient to satisfy their tax liability and also to provide full-time care and assistance to their dependent child, who has a serious long-term illness. The unpaid taxes were a result of the Snyders providing needed medical care for their sick child. They will need to continue to use their assets to provide for basic living expenses and ongoing medical care for the child. There is no doubt that the tax is correct, but to pay the tax now would endanger the life of their child and would create a serious hardship.

In order to apply for an OIC, a taxpayer must submit a $150 application fee and initial nonrefundable payment along with Form 656, *Offer in Compromise*.

For the initial payment, the taxpayer has two options:

1) The taxpayer may submit 20% of the total offer and wait for an acceptance from the IRS, and then pay the remaining balance of the offer in five or fewer installments.
2) The taxpayer can submit an initial payment with the application and continue to pay the remaining balance in monthly installments while the IRS is reviewing the offer. Once accepted, the taxpayer will continue monthly installments until the liability is satisfied.

The taxpayer may appeal a rejected offer in compromise within 30 days.

In 2012 the IRS published new guidelines for its OIC program, as part of its "Fresh Start" initiative to help taxpayers resolve delinquent federal tax liabilities. The new OIC guidelines change the way the IRS calculates a taxpayer's ability to pay. The changes are expected to significantly increase the number of taxpayers who qualify for an OIC.

Unit 7: Questions

1. All of the following are types of relief from joint and several liability for spouses who file joint returns except:

A. Innocent spouse relief.
B. Separation of liability relief.
C. Joint relief.
D. Equitable relief.

The answer is C. There is no such thing as "joint relief." There are three types of relief from joint and several liability for spouses who file joint returns: innocent spouse relief, separation of liability relief, and equitable relief. ###

2. A levy allows the IRS to _____.

A. Confiscate and sell property to satisfy a tax debt.
B. Publicly notify a taxpayer's creditors of a claim against his property.
C. Collect tax beyond the statute of limitations.
D. Sell property on behalf of the taxpayer.

The answer is A. A levy allows the IRS to confiscate and sell property to satisfy a tax debt. An IRS levy refers to the actual seizing of property authorized by an earlier filed tax lien. Answer "B" refers to a lien, which gives the IRS a legal claim to a taxpayer's property as security for his tax debt. ###

3. How does the IRS begin the process of collections?

A. With an email to the taxpayer as soon as he files his tax return.
B. With a certified letter to the taxpayer immediately after a tax return is processed and flagged for audit.
C. With a written examination notice when the taxpayer is notified of the possibility of an audit.
D. A first notice will be sent, which is a letter that explains the balance due and demands payment in full.

The answer is D. If a taxpayer does not pay in full when filing his tax return, he will receive a bill from an IRS service center. The first notice will be a letter that explains the balance due and demands payment in full. It will include the amount of the tax plus any penalties and interest added to the taxpayer's unpaid balance from the date the tax was due. ###

4. All of the following statements about the IRS statute of limitations are true except:

A. The IRS generally has ten years following an assessment to begin proceedings to collect the tax by levy or in a court proceeding.
B. The IRS is required to notify the taxpayer that he may refuse to extend the statute of limitations.
C. The taxpayer may not choose to extend the statute of limitations.
D. IRS Form 872-A indefinitely extends the time that a tax may be assessed.

The answer is C. The taxpayer may choose to extend the statute of limitations by signing Form 872-A. The taxpayer also may refuse to extend the statute. If a taxpayer does not file a tax return, the statute of limitations does not expire. The statute of limitations on collection may also be suspended by various acts. ###

5. The IRS may accept an offer in compromise based on three grounds. All of the following are valid grounds for submitting an OIC to the IRS except:

A. Doubt as to collectability.
B. Effective tax administration.
C. Legitimate shelter argument.
D. Doubt as to liability.

The answer is C. The IRS may accept an OIC based on three grounds: doubt as to collectability, effective tax administration, and doubt as to liability. ###

6. The statute of limitations on collection can be suspended by various acts. The ten-year collection period may be suspended in each of the following cases except:

A. While the IRS and the Office of Appeals consider a request for an installment agreement or an offer in compromise.
B. From the date a taxpayer requests a collection due process (CDP) hearing.
C. While the taxpayer is in prison.
D. While the taxpayer lives outside the United States.

The answer is C. The ten-year collection period is not suspended when a taxpayer is in prison. The ten-year collection period is suspended in the following cases:
- While the IRS considers a request for an installment agreement or an offer in compromise
- From the date a taxpayer requests a collection due process (CDP) hearing
- For tax periods included in a bankruptcy
- While the taxpayer is residing outside the United States

The amount of time the suspension is in effect will be added to the time remaining in the ten-year period. For example, if the ten-year period is suspended for six months, the time left in the period the IRS has to collect will increase by six months. ###

7. Separation of liability relief does not apply to taxpayers who are _____.

A. Divorced.
B. Legally separated.
C. Widowed.
D. Single (never married).

The answer is D. In order to qualify for separation of liability relief, the taxpayer must have filed a joint return. That means that the taxpayer must have been married at one time. Separation of liability applies to taxpayers who are:
(1)No longer married, or
(2)Legally separated, or
(3)Living apart for the 12 months prior to the filing of a claim.
Under this rule, a taxpayer also qualifies if the taxpayer is widowed. "Living apart" does not include a spouse who is only temporarily absent from the household. ###

8. A taxpayer may qualify as an injured spouse if _____.

A. He files a joint return and his share of the refund was applied against past due amounts owed by a spouse.
B. He files a joint return and fails to report income.
C. He files a separate return and has the refund offset by past student loan obligations.
D. He files for bankruptcy protection.

The answer is A. A taxpayer may qualify as an injured spouse if he files a joint return and his share of the refund was applied against past due amounts owed by a spouse. The injured spouse may be entitled to recoup only his share of a tax refund. ###

9. Ingrid requests innocent spouse relief in 2012. While Ingrid's request is pending, which of the following is true?

A. The IRS may still enforce collection action.
B. Interest and penalties do not continue to accrue.
C. Tax shelter penalties may apply.
D. Collection action must cease while the taxpayer's request is being considered.

The answer is D. If a taxpayer requests innocent spouse relief, the IRS cannot enforce collection action while the taxpayer's request is pending. However, interest and penalties continue to accrue. The request is generally considered pending from the date it is received by the IRS until the date the innocent spouse request is resolved. ###

10. Belinda and Neil file jointly. They report $15,000 of income and deductions, but Belinda knew that Neil was not reporting $3,000 of dividends. The income is not hers and she has no access to it since it is in Neil's bank account. She signs the joint return. The return is later chosen for examination, and penalties are assessed. Does Belinda qualify for innocent spouse relief?

A. Belinda is not eligible for innocent spouse relief because she knew about the understated tax.
B. Belinda is eligible for innocent spouse relief because she had no control over the income.
C. Belinda is eligible for injured spouse relief.
D. None of the above.

The answer is A. Belinda is not eligible for innocent spouse relief because she knew about the understated tax. She signed the return knowing that the income was not included, so she cannot apply for relief (Publication 971). ###

11. The IRS may legally seize property in which of the following circumstances?

A. During the consideration of an offer in compromise.
B. If the collection of tax is in jeopardy.
C. If the taxpayer's liability is $5,000 or less in a seizure of real property (real estate).
D. While innocent spouse claims are pending.

The answer is B. The IRS may still seize or levy property if the collection of tax is in jeopardy. Typically, the IRS may not seize property in the following circumstances:
•When there is a pending installment agreement
•While a taxpayer's appeal is pending
•During the consideration of an offer in compromise
•During a bankruptcy (*unless* the seizure is authorized by the bankruptcy court)
•If the taxpayer's liability is $5,000 or less in a seizure of real property (real estate)
•While innocent spouse claims are pending
Judicial approval is required for most principal residence seizures. The IRS may still seize or levy property if the collection of tax is in jeopardy. ###

12. Lena owes $20,000 for unpaid federal tax liabilities. She agrees she owes the tax, but she has a serious medical problem and her monthly income does not meet her necessary living expenses. She does not own any real estate and does not have the ability to fully pay the liability now or through monthly installment payments. What type of relief may she qualify for?

A. Doubt as to collectability.
B. Doubt as to liability.
C. Effective tax administration.
D. Collection advocate procedure.

The answer is A. Lena may apply for an offer in compromise under doubt as to collectability. Doubt exists that she could ever pay the full amount of tax liability owed within the remainder of the statutory period for collection. ###

13. A taxpayer may appeal IRS collection actions to the IRS Office of Appeals. The two main appeal procedures are:

A. Offer in compromise and doubt as to collection.
B. Collection due process and the collection appeals program.
C. Collection due process and the U.S. Tax Court Program.
D. Taxpayer Advocate Service and the collection appeals program.

The answer is B. The two main appeal procedures for IRS collection action are collection due process and the collection appeals program. ###

14. All of the following property is exempt from an IRS levy except:

A. Undelivered mail.
B. Child support payments.
C. Social Security payments.
D. Unemployment benefits.

The answer is C. Regular Social Security payments are not exempt from IRS levy. ###

15. Beverly wants to submit an offer in compromise to the IRS. In which of the following circumstances is she not required to send an initial payment along with her application?

A. Doubt as to collectability.
B. Effective tax administration.
C. Doubt as to liability.
D. An initial payment is always required, in addition to the application fee.

The answer is C. If a taxpayer submits an OIC under doubt as to liability, no payment is required with the submission. ###

16. Which statement is correct regarding the collection appeals process?

A. The decision in a collection due process hearing is final, and a taxpayer may not appeal even if he is unhappy with the determination.
B. A disposition in the collection appeals program is typically slower than in a CDP, but the taxpayer has the right to appeal if he is unhappy with a CAP determination.
C. Innocent spouse relief may not be discussed during a CDP hearing.
D. If a taxpayer disagrees with the Appeals officer's determination after a CDP hearing, he can appeal to another court.

The answer is D. In a collection due process hearing, the taxpayer retains the right to appeal, unlike in the collection appeals program where the determination is final. Innocent spouse relief may be a topic of discussion in a CDP, along with many other issues. ###

17. If a taxpayer believes the IRS is not handling its case in a timely and appropriate manner, he should contact the _____ for assistance.

A. The IRS Help Line.
B. The U.S. Tax Court.
C. The Taxpayer Advocate Service.
D. The IRS Appeals office.

The answer is C. Congress created the Taxpayer Advocate Service, an independent entity within the IRS, to help taxpayers resolve issues with the IRS and recommend changes that will prevent future problems. Every year, the TAS helps thousands of taxpayers find solutions to their tax issues. There is no charge to taxpayers to use the service. ###

Unit 8: The IRS Examination Process

> **More Reading:**
> Publication 556, *Examination of Returns, Appeal Rights, and Claims for Refund*
> Publication 1, *Your Rights as a Taxpayer*
> Publication 3498, *The Examination Process*

The IRS accepts most tax returns as they are filed, but selects a small percentage for examination.[52] In 2012, the IRS audited 1.03% of the total number of individual tax returns with a filing requirement, down slightly from the 2011 percentage. Higher income earners were audited much more heavily than those who earned less. The IRS reports the audit rate for returns with total positive income of $1 million or more was 12.14%.[53] Of the individual returns audited in 2011, nearly a third were for returns with EIC claims. [54]

An IRS examination is a review of an organization's or individual's accounts and financial information to ensure information is being reported correctly and according to the tax laws, and to verify the amount of tax reported is accurate. The IRS will contact a taxpayer by telephone or mail only, due to disclosure requirements. E-mail notification is not used by the IRS.

Selecting a return for examination does not necessarily suggest that the taxpayer has made an error or been dishonest. Filing an amended return does not affect the selection process of the original return. However, amended returns also go through a screening process and an amended return may be selected for audit.

The responsibility to prove entries, deductions, and statements made on a tax return is known as the "burden of proof." The taxpayer must be able to substantiate expenses in order to deduct them. Taxpayers can usually meet their burden of proof by having the receipts for the expenses.

A tax return may be examined for multiple reasons. After the examination, if any change to the taxpayer's return is proposed, he can disagree with the chang-

---

[52] Even though the IRS uses the term "examination" rather than "audit," the terms mean essentially the same thing.
[53] The Kiplinger Tax Letter, Vol. 88, No. 2.
[54] IR-2012-36, The IRS Data Book.

es and appeal the IRS's decision. This is done through the appeals process, which we'll cover in Unit 9. In this study unit, we'll cover the examination process.

The IRS conducts most examinations entirely by mail. In these "correspondence audits,"[55] a taxpayer will receive a letter asking for additional information about certain items shown on the return, such as proof of income, expens-expenses, and itemized deductions.

Correspondence audits occur typically when there is a minor issue that the IRS needs to clarify. Sometimes, the IRS is simply requesting proof that a particular transaction has transpired.

Example: The IRS sends Pete a notice about his 2011 tax return. He had disposed of a large number of stocks during the year, and the IRS wanted basis information on them. Pete requests a report from his stockbroker showing the basis and sends it to the IRS along with a copy of the notice. The issue is resolved without incident, and Pete receives a notice showing that no changes have been made to his tax return.

Example: The IRS selects Sarah's return for examination. Sarah had claimed her older half-sister as a "qualifying child" based on her permanent disability, and also claimed head of household status. The IRS asks for proof of disability and residency, and Sarah provides copies of doctors' records and additional proof that her sister lived with her full-time. The IRS accepts Sarah's documents and closes the case as a "no change" audit. Sarah never has to meet with the IRS auditor, as the entire audit is conducted by mail (Publication 3498).

Taxpayer Rights During the Examination Process

The taxpayer has a number of rights during the IRS examination process. These rights include:

- A right to professional and courteous treatment by IRS employees
- A right to privacy and confidentiality about tax matters
- A right to know why the IRS is asking for information, how the IRS will use it, and what will happen if the requested information is not provided
- A right to representation, either by oneself or an authorized representative

---

[55] In fiscal year 2011, 75% of all examinations were correspondence audits (IRS Data Book).

- A right to appeal disagreements, both within the IRS and before the courts

How Returns are Selected for Examination

The IRS selects returns for examination using a variety of methods, including:

- **Potential Abusive/Tax Avoidance Transactions:** Some returns are selected based on information obtained by the IRS through efforts to identify promoters and participants of abusive tax avoidance transactions.
- **Computer Scoring/DIF Score:** Other tax returns may be chosen for examination on the basis of computer scoring. A computer program called the "Discriminant Inventory Function System" (DIF) assigns a numeric score to each individual and some corporate tax returns after they have been processed. [56]
- **Information Matching:** Some returns are examined because payer reports, such as Forms W-2 from employers or Form 1099 interest statements from banks, do not match the income reported on the tax return. The return may also be selected for examination on the basis of information received from third-party documentation that may conflict with the information reported on the tax return.
- **Related Examinations:** Returns may be selected for audit when they involve issues or transactions with other taxpayers, such as business partners or investors, whose returns were selected for examination.
- **Third Party Information:** A return may be selected as a result of information received from other third-party sources or individuals. This information can come from a number of sources, including state and local law enforcement agencies, public records, and individuals. The information is evaluated for reliability and accuracy before it is used as the basis of an examination or investigation.

---

[56] IRS computers automatically check tax returns and assign a "DIF score" based on the probability that the return contains errors, excessive tax deductions, or other issues. This does not necessarily mean that the return was prepared incorrectly. However, the computer is trained to look for aberrations and questionable items. If a taxpayer's return is selected because of a high score under the DIF system, the return has a high probability of being chosen for audit. The IRS does not release information about how it calculates a taxpayer's DIF score.

Example: Perry is an EA with a client, Lila, who received an audit notice this year. Lila's tax return was selected because she had a very high number of credits and very little taxable income. However, her tax return was prepared correctly. Lila had adopted four special-needs children in 2012 and was able to take a large adoption credit. Perry provided proof of the adoptions to the examining officer, which resulted in a positive outcome for Lila and a "no-change" audit.

Example: Van embezzled money from his employer and was arrested in 2012 for felony embezzlement. The case was made public and the police shared their information with the IRS. The IRS then contacted Van and made an adjustment to all of his tax returns, assessing additional tax, interest, and penalties for fraud for failing to report the embezzled funds as income. This is an example of third party information that can trigger an IRS investigation.

Notice of IRS Contact of Third Parties

During the examination process, the IRS may contact third parties regarding a tax matter without the taxpayer's permission. The IRS may contact third parties such as neighbors, banks, employers, or employees.

The IRS must give the taxpayer reasonable notice before contacting other persons about his individual tax matters.

The IRS must provide the taxpayer with a record of persons contacted on both a periodic basis and upon the taxpayer's request. This provision does not apply:

- To any pending criminal investigation
- When providing notice would jeopardize collection of any tax liability
- When providing notice may result in reprisal against any person
- When the taxpayer has already authorized the contact

Example: Max's tax return was selected by the IRS for audit. The IRS suspects unreported income due to criminal drug activity. Max is also being investigated by the FBI. Because this is a pending criminal investigation, the IRS is not required to give Max reasonable notice before contacting third parties about his individual tax matters.

Repeat Examinations

The IRS tries to avoid repeat examinations of the same items, but sometimes this happens. If a taxpayer's return was audited for the same items in the previous two years and no change was proposed to tax liability, the taxpayer may contact the IRS and request that the examination be discontinued.

Example: Kelly donates a large percentage of her salary to her church. For the last two years, the IRS has selected Kelly's return for examination based on her large donations. In both instances, Kelly was able to substantiate her donations and "no change" was made to her tax liability. Kelly's tax return is selected again for the same reason in 2012. Kelly contacts the IRS to request that the examination be discontinued, and the examining officer agrees to do so.

Example: Santiago's tax return has been selected for examination three years in a row. In 2010 and 2011, his tax return was selected to verify compliance for the EIC. There was no change to his tax liability in either year. In 2012, Santiago's tax return is selected for audit again. This time, the IRS is questioning his education deductions. Santiago cannot request that the examination be discontinued because it is for a different item than in the previous two examinations.

The Audit Location

The IRS chooses to conduct some audits face-to-face, which are known as field audits. Examinations that are not handled by mail may take place at:

- The taxpayer's home or place of business
- An IRS office
- The office of the taxpayer's authorized representative (attorney, CPA, or enrolled agent)

Most often, a taxpayer's return is examined in the area where he lives. But if the return can be examined more conveniently in another area, such as where the taxpayer's records are located, he may request the audit be transferred to that area.

The IRS must make exceptions for extenuating circumstances. For example, if the taxpayer is currently on active duty in a combat zone, the examination must be temporarily suspended. However, the IRS will make the final determination of when, where, and how the examination will take place.

177

Example: Joyce runs a marketing business, and she travels frequently in order to promote her business. She lives in Los Angeles; however, her CPA is in Chicago. In 2012 Joyce's tax return is selected for examination and she chooses to have her CPA represent her. Her CPA requests that the examination be transferred to Chicago where Joyce's records are located. The transfer is granted.

During the Examination

In examinations not handled by mail, the taxpayer or the taxpayer's representative must make an appointment to meet with the IRS. The examining officer will notify the taxpayer of any records that are required. The IRS officer must explain any proposed changes to the taxpayer's return.

The IRS must follow the tax laws set forth by Congress in the Internal Revenue Code. The IRS also follows court decisions, but the IRS may choose to disregard[57] a court decision on the same issue and still apply its own interpretation of tax law.

If the taxpayer agrees with the IRS's proposed changes, he may immediately sign an agreement. The taxpayer is responsible for paying interest on any additional tax. If the taxpayer pays any additional tax owed when he signs the agreement, the interest is figured from the due date of the tax return to the date of the payment.

If the taxpayer does not pay the additional tax when he signs the agreement, he will receive a bill that includes interest. If the taxpayer pays the amount due within ten business days of the billing date, he will not have to pay any more interest or penalties. This period is extended to 21 calendar days if the amount due is less than $100,000.

If the taxpayer is due a refund, he will receive the refund sooner if he signs the agreement. The taxpayer will be paid interest on the refund. If the IRS accepts the tax return as filed (a no-change audit), the taxpayer will receive a confirmation letter stating that the IRS proposed no changes to the return.

---

[57]The IRS may choose whether or not to "acquiesce" to a court decision. This means that the IRS may choose to ignore the decision of the court and continue with its regular policies regarding the litigated issue. This concept is covered in more detail later.

Audit Determinations

An audit can be closed in three ways:

- **No change:** An audit in which the taxpayer has substantiated all of the items being reviewed and it results in no changes.
- **Agreed:** An audit in which the IRS proposes changes and the taxpayer understands and agrees with the changes.
- **Disagreed:** An audit in which the IRS proposes changes and the taxpayer understands, but disagrees with the changes. A conference with a manager may be requested for further review of the issue. In addition, the taxpayer may request fast track mediation or an appeal. The taxpayer may also choose to go to court and contest the IRS's determination (both appeals and the court system are covered in detail in Unit 9).

The IRS will not typically reopen a closed examination case to make an unfavorable adjustment unless:

- There was fraud or misrepresentation
- There was a substantial error based on an established IRS position existing at the time of the examination, or
- Failure to reopen the case would be a serious administrative omission.

The Taxpayer's Representative

A taxpayer is always allowed to use a qualified representative before the IRS. The taxpayer does not have to attend the audit if the representative has proper authorization from the taxpayer and is an authorized representative (an "enrolled practitioner" per Circular 230). If the taxpayer chooses to use a representative, he may be any federally authorized practitioner, including an attorney, a CPA, or an EA. The taxpayer may also choose to have a close family member represent him.

Example: Astrid is an EA. A taxpayer named Seth hires her to represent him before the IRS during the examination of his tax return. Seth does not want to attend the audit. He signs Form 2848 indicating that Astrid is now his authorized representative for all his tax affairs. Astrid attends the examination on Seth's behalf.

Representatives must have prior written authorization in order to represent the taxpayer before the IRS. Representatives may use Form 2848, *Power of Attorney and Declaration of Representative*.

The taxpayer may always represent himself during an examination. If during the audit he becomes uncomfortable and wishes to consult with a tax advisor, the IRS must suspend the interview and reschedule it. However, the IRS will not suspend the interview if the taxpayer is there because of an administrative summons.

On a jointly filed tax return that is selected for examination, only one spouse is required to meet with the IRS.

Limited Confidentiality Privilege

Taxpayers are granted a confidentiality privilege with any federally authorized practitioner (usually, a CPA, EA, or attorney). Confidential communications include:

- Advising the taxpayer on tax matters within the scope of the practitioner's authority to practice before the IRS,
- Communications that would be confidential between an attorney and the taxpayer, and
  - Relate to *noncriminal* tax matters before the IRS, or
  - Relate to *noncriminal* tax proceedings brought in federal court by or against the United States.[58]

The confidentiality privilege does not apply to communications in connection with the promotion of or participation in a tax shelter. A tax shelter is any entity, plan, or arrangement whose significant purpose is to avoid or evade income tax. The confidentiality privilege also does not apply to issues related to any other branch of government.

This privilege is not applicable to the preparation and filing of a tax return. Nor does the privilege apply to state tax matters, although a number of states have an accountant-client privilege.

---

[58] See IRS Publication 556.

The IRS must allow taxpayers to claim the confidentiality privilege in communications with a federally authorized tax practitioner. The taxpayer or representative must assert the confidentiality privilege; it does not arise automatically.

Recording the Audit Interview

The practitioner may record the examination interview. The practitioner must notify the examiner ten days in advance in writing that he wishes to record the interview. The IRS may also record an interview. If the IRS initiates the recording, the taxpayer and/or the representative must be notified ten days in advance, and the taxpayer may request a copy of the recording.

Suspension of Interest and Penalties Due to IRS Delays

The IRS has three years from the date the taxpayer filed his return (or the date the return was due, if later) to assess any additional tax. This rule applies even if a tax return is filed late. The IRS cannot assess additional tax or issue a refund or credit after the statute of limitations has expired.

The IRS must send a taxpayer a notice explaining any additional liability. However, if the taxpayer files his return timely (including extensions), interest and certain penalties will be *suspended* if the IRS fails to mail a notice to the taxpayer stating:

- The taxpayer's liability, and
- The basis for that liability.

Penalties and interest will not be suspended in the following cases:

- The failure-to-pay penalty
- Any fraudulent tax return
- Any amount related to a gross misstatement
- Any amount related to a reportable transaction (a tax shelter) that was not adequately disclosed
- Any listed transaction
- Any criminal penalty

The IRS will waive penalties when allowed by law if the taxpayer can show that he acted in good faith or relied on the incorrect advice of an IRS employee.

Requesting Abatement of Interest Due to IRS Error or Delay

The IRS will waive interest that is the result of certain errors or delays caused by an IRS employee. The IRS will abate the interest only if there was an unreasonable error or delay in performing a managerial or ministerial act (defined below). The taxpayer cannot have caused any significant aspect of the error or delay. In addition, the interest can be abated only if it relates to taxes for which a Notice of Deficiency is required.

Managerial Act

The term "managerial act" means an administrative act that occurs during the processing of the taxpayer's case involving the temporary or permanent loss of records or the exercise of judgment or discretion relating to management of personnel. The proper application of federal tax law is not a managerial act.

Ministerial Act

The term "ministerial act" means a procedural or mechanical act that does not involve the exercise of judgment or discretion and that occurs during the processing of the taxpayer's case after all prerequisites of the act, such as conferences and review by supervisors, have taken place. The proper application of federal tax law is not a ministerial act.

Example: Calvin moves to another state before the IRS selects his tax return for examination. A letter stating that Calvin's return was selected for examination was sent to his old address and then forwarded to his new address. When he gets the letter, he responds with a request that the examination be transferred to the area office closest to his new address. The examination group manager approves his request. However, the original examination manager forgets about the transfer and fails to transfer the file for six months. The transfer is a ministerial act. The IRS can reduce the interest Calvin owes because of any unreasonable delay in transferring the case.

Example: A revenue agent is examining Margaret's tax return. During the course of the examination, the agent is sent to an extended training course. The agent's supervisor decides not to reassign the audit case, so the examination is unreasonably delayed until the agent returns. Interest caused by the unreasonable delay can be abated since the decision to send the agent to the training class and the decision not to reassign the case are both managerial acts.

A taxpayer may request an abatement of interest on Form 843, *Claim for Refund and Request for Abatement.* The taxpayer should file the claim with the IRS service center where the examination was affected by the error or delay. If a request for abatement of interest is denied, an appeal can be made to the IRS Appeals Office and the U.S. Tax Court.

Special Rules for Partnership (TEFRA) Examinations

IRS audits of partnerships can be complicated since partnerships are regarded as pass-through entities, and do not pay tax on the income they report. Income, gain, loss, deductions, and credits are all reported on the partners' individual tax returns, not as a partnership as a whole.

When a question arises about the accuracy of a partnership return, it may be impractical for the IRS to audit each individual partner's return. Under the Tax Equity and Fiscal Responsibility Act of 1982 (TEFRA), the IRS will first audit the partnership as a single entity, with a "tax matters partner" (TMP) serving as the main contact.

IRS examiners will attempt to determine whether partnership losses were properly treated and recorded. If the IRS determines that losses were not properly treated, it will assess tax at the partnership level. The TMP would then decide whether to appeal the decision.

There is an exception under TEFRA for small partnerships consisting of ten or fewer partners. These partnerships may still elect, however, to be covered by the TEFRA provisions.

IRS examiners have strict procedures to follow during a TEFRA audit, including mandatory completion of check sheets to detail correct procedures.

Unit 8: Questions

1. Frank's tax return was chosen by the IRS for examination. He moved a few months ago to another state, but the IRS notice says that his examination will be scheduled in the city where he used to live. Which of the following statements is true about this issue?

A. Frank can request that his tax return examination be moved to another IRS service center since he has moved to another area.
B. Frank must schedule the examination in his former city of residence, but he can have a professional represent him.
C. Frank is required to meet with the auditor at least once in person in order to move the examination to another location.
D. None of the above.

The answer is A. If a taxpayer has moved or if his books and records are located in another area, he can request that the location of his audit be changed to another IRS service center. ###

2. On a jointly filed tax return that has been selected for examination, which of the following statements is true?

A. Both spouses must be present during an examination, because both spouses signed the return.
B. Only one spouse must be present.
C. Neither spouse must respond to the notice.
D. Neither spouse may use a representative.

The answer is B. For taxpayers who file jointly, only one spouse is required to meet with the IRS. The taxpayers can also choose to use a qualified representative to represent them before the IRS. ###

3. When a taxpayer is chosen for an IRS audit, which of the following statements is true?

A. The taxpayer must appear before the IRS in person.
B. A taxpayer may choose to be represented before the IRS and is not required to appear if he so wishes.
C. An audit case may not be transferred to a different IRS office under any circumstances.
D. If a taxpayer feels that he is not being treated fairly during an IRS audit, he cannot appeal to the auditor's manager.

The answer is B. The taxpayer is not required to be present during an IRS examination if he has provided written authorization to a qualified representative per Circular 230. ###

4. What is a DIF score?

A. A computer scoring process that the IRS uses to select some returns for audit.
B. A report that is transmitted with each filed return.
C. A score that an auditor gives to the tax practitioner.
D. An IRS scoring process for Tax Court procedures.

The answer is A. The Discriminant Inventory Function System (DIF) score rates potential returns for audit, based on past IRS experience with similar returns. IRS personnel screen the highest-scoring returns, selecting some for audit and identifying the items on these returns that are most likely to need review. ###

5. The IRS must give the taxpayer reasonable notice before contacting other persons about his individual tax matters. The IRS must also provide the taxpayer with a record of persons contacted on both a periodic basis and upon the taxpayer's request. This provision does not apply:

A. To any pending criminal investigation.
B. When providing notice would jeopardize collection of any tax liability.
C. When providing notice may result in reprisal against any person.
D. All of the above.

The answer is D. During the examination process, the IRS must give the taxpayer reasonable notice before contacting other persons about his individual tax matters. This provision does not apply:

- To any pending criminal investigation.
- When providing notice would jeopardize collection of any tax liability.
- When providing notice may result in reprisal against any person.
- When the taxpayer has already authorized the contact. ###

6. Taxpayers are granted a confidentiality privilege with any federally authorized practitioner. This is the same confidentiality protection that a taxpayer would have with an attorney, with some exceptions. Confidential communications include all of the following except:

A. Written tax advice.
B. Matters that would be confidential between an attorney and a client.
C. Participation in a tax shelter.
D. Noncriminal tax matters before the IRS.

The answer is C. The confidentiality privilege does not apply in the case of communications regarding the promotion of or participation in a tax shelter. A tax shelter is any entity, plan, or arrangement whose significant purpose is to avoid or evade income tax. ###

7. According to the IRS, tax returns are selected for audit based on a number of different reasons. All of the following are reasons a return may be chosen for audit except:

A. Potential abusive transactions.
B. Computer scoring.
C. Because the taxpayer is a foreign investor.
D. Information received from other third-party sources or individuals.

The answer is C. A taxpayer would not be chosen for audit simply because he is a foreign investor. The IRS selects returns using a variety of methods, including potential participants in abusive tax avoidance transactions; computer scoring; information matching (some returns are examined because payer reports such as Forms W-2 from employers or Form 1099 interest statements from banks do not match the income reported on the tax return); related examinations (related entities may be audited together); or local compliance projects (random audits). ###

8. Does filing an amended return affect a tax return's audit selection?

A. Filing an amended return does not affect the selection process of the original return.
B. Filing an amended return always affects the selection process of the original return.
C. An amended return is MORE likely to be selected for an IRS audit.
D. An amended return is LESS likely to be selected for an IRS audit.

The answer is A. Filing an amended return does not affect the selection process of the original return. However, amended returns go through a screening process and an amended return may be selected for audit, just like any other return. ###

9. In general, the IRS will not reopen a closed examination case. All of the following are reasons why the IRS would reopen a closed audit case except:

A. There was fraud or misrepresentation.
B. There was a substantial error based on an established IRS position existing at the time of the examination.
C. Failure to reopen the case would be a serious administrative omission.
D. The taxpayer filed a request for fast track mediation.

The answer is D. Requesting fast track mediation during the examination is not a reason for the IRS to reopen a closed audit case. In general, the IRS will not reopen a closed examination case to make an unfavorable adjustment unless:

• There was fraud or misrepresentation,
• There was a substantial error based on an established IRS position existing at the time of the examination, or
• Failure to reopen the case would be a serious administrative omission.

###

10. The IRS has begun an examination of Elaine's income tax return. The IRS would like to ask her neighbors questions related to the examination. There is no pending criminal investigation into the matter, and there is no evidence that such contact will result in reprisals against the neighbors or jeopardize collection of the tax liability. Before contacting the neighbors, the IRS must:

A. Provide Elaine with reasonable notice of the contact.
B. Make an assessment of Elaine's tax liability.
C. Ask the court for a third-party record keeper subpoena.
D. Mail Elaine a Statutory Notice of Deficiency.

The answer is A. Pursuant to IRC §7602(c), a third-party contact is made when an IRS employee initiates contact with a person other than the taxpayer. A third party may be contacted to obtain information about a specific taxpayer's federal tax liability, including the issuance of a levy or summons to someone other than the taxpayer. The IRS does not need permission to contact third parties, but it must notify the taxpayer that the contact with third parties will be made. ###

11. The IRS will close an audit in all of the following situations except:

A. When there's a recommendation of no change.
B. When the taxpayer disagrees with the IRS's conclusions and requests fast track mediation.
C. When the IRS contacts the county district attorney and recommends criminal prosecution.
D. When the IRS proposes changes and the taxpayer agrees.

The answer is C. An audit can be closed with "no change;" "agreed" (as in Answer D); or "disagreed" (as in Answer B in which the IRS proposes changes and the taxpayer disagrees. He may then ask for further review, request fast track mediation, or pursue an appeal with the IRS or the judicial system.) Answer C is incorrect. If criminal prosecution resulted from an IRS audit, it would not be pursued by a county district attorney and the audit would not be closed. ###

12. If a taxpayer or his representative wishes for an audit to be recorded, which of the following must he do?

A. Make a request the same day as the examination.
B. Notify the examiner ten days in advance, in writing.
C. Notify the examiner one week in advance, in writing.
D. Nothing. All examinations are automatically recorded by the IRS to ensure compliance of regulations by all parties.

The answer is B. If a taxpayer, his representative, or the IRS examiner wishes for an audit to be recorded, he must notify the other parties in writing ten days in advance. If the IRS records the interview, the taxpayer may request a copy. ###

13. When the IRS needs to examine the records of a partnership, it must do so under the rules of TEFRA. All of the following statements are correct except:

A. Partnerships with more than ten partners are exempt from the TEFRA rules.
B. Because TEFRA audits are so complicated, the IRS must follow special procedures when it initiates and conducts examinations.
C. A tax matters partner will be the main contact with examiners during a TEFRA audit.
D. Under TEFRA, the IRS will examine tax issues at the partnership level, rather than examine each individual partner's return.

The answer is A. "A" is incorrect because partnerships with ten partners or fewer are typically exempt from the TEFRA rules under a special small partnership exception. ###

Unit 9: The Appeals Process

More Reading:
Publication 5, *Your Appeal Rights*
Publication 556, *Examination of Returns, Appeal Rights, and Claims for Refund*
Publication 4227, *Overview of the Appeals Process*
Publication 4167, *Appeals: Introduction to Alternative Dispute Resolution*

Because taxpayers often disagree with the IRS on tax matters, the IRS has an appeal system. Every taxpayer has the right to appeal changes on a tax return that is audited. Most differences are settled within the appeals system without going to court.

The Appeals Office is *independent* of any other IRS office and serves as an informal administrative forum for any taxpayer who disagrees with an IRS determination. Appeals is a venue where disagreements concerning the application of tax law can be resolved on an impartial basis for both the taxpayer and the government. The mission of Appeals is to settle tax disagreements without having to go to the courts and a formal trial.

Reasons for an appeal must be supported by tax law, however. An appeal of a case cannot be based solely on moral, religious, political, constitutional, conscientious, or similar grounds.

If the taxpayer chooses not to appeal within the IRS system, he may take his case directly to the U.S. Tax Court. The tax does not have to be paid first in order to appeal within the IRS or to the U.S. Tax Court.

The taxpayer may opt to bypass both the IRS appeals process and the Tax Court and instead take his case to the U.S. Court of Federal Claims or a local U.S. district court. However, if the taxpayer chooses to go directly to the Court of Federal Claims or a U.S. district court, all of the contested tax must first be paid. The taxpayer must then sue the IRS for a refund.

Only enrolled preparers (usually, attorneys, CPAs, or EAs) are allowed to represent taxpayers before an appeals hearing.

Taxpayer Appeal Rights

During the IRS appeals and examination process, taxpayers have the right to:

- Disagree with their tax bill
- Meet with an IRS manager
- Appeal most IRS collection actions
- Have their cases transferred to a different IRS office if they have a valid reason, such as if they have moved to another city
- Be represented by an agent (such as a CPA, EA, or attorney) when dealing with IRS matters
- Receive a receipt for any payment made to the IRS

Starting the Appeals Process

At the beginning of each examination, the IRS auditor must explain a taxpayer's appeal rights. If the taxpayer chooses to appeal the examiner's decision through the IRS system, he can file an appeal at a local IRS appeals office, which is a separate entity from local IRS district offices. He will then receive a letter from the IRS, which sets a time limit to file for an appeal conference.

The appeals procedure varies based on the amount of the proposed tax. If the amount is less than $2,500, the taxpayer must only contact the IRS to initiate an appeal. If the amount is more than $2,500 but less than $10,000, a brief statement of disputed tax is required. If the disputed amount exceeds $10,000, then a formal written protest is required.

An IRS appeal does not abate penalties and interest on the tax due. They continue to accumulate until the balance of the debt is paid, or until the taxpayer wins his appeal and he is granted a no-change audit, meaning the IRS has accepted the tax return as it was filed, and no additional tax is due.

30-Day Letter and 90-Day Letter

Proposed Individual Tax Assessment: The 30-Day Letter

Within a few weeks after a taxpayer's closing conference with an IRS examiner, he will receive a Proposed Individual Tax Assessment (more commonly called the **"30-day letter"**). This letter includes:

- A notice explaining the taxpayer's right to appeal the proposed changes within 30 days
- A copy of the examination report explaining the examiner's proposed changes
- An agreement or waiver form
- A copy of Publication 5, *Your Appeal Rights and How to Prepare a Protest If You Don't Agree*

The taxpayer has 30 days from the date of notice to accept or appeal the proposed changes.

Statutory Notice of Deficiency: The 90-Day Letter

If the taxpayer does not respond to the 30-day letter or if he cannot reach an agreement with an appeals officer, the IRS will send the taxpayer a 90-day letter, which is also known as a "Statutory Notice of Deficiency." A Notice of Deficiency is required by law and is used to advise the taxpayer of his appeal rights to the U.S. Tax Court.

A Notice of Deficiency must be issued before a taxpayer can go to Tax Court. This means that the taxpayer must wait for the IRS to send him a "final notice" before he can petition the Tax Court to hear his case. The taxpayer will have 90 days (150 days if addressed to a taxpayer outside the United States) from the date of this notice to file a petition with the Tax Court.

If the taxpayer does not file the petition in time, the tax is due within ten days, and the taxpayer may not take his case to Tax Court.

If the taxpayer does file a petition in time and the case becomes docketed before Tax Court, his file will again go to an appeals office to see if it can be resolved before it goes to Tax Court. Over 90% of all tax cases are solved before going to Tax Court.

During the examination and appeals process, taxpayers always have the burden of proving their deductions and their income. However, with alleged "unreported income," the IRS has the burden of proof based on any reconstruction of income solely through the use of statistical information on unrelated taxpayers.

> **Example:** Ken owns a cash-only business and the IRS disagrees with his stated income. The IRS reconstructs Ken's income based on industry standards, but does not have actual proof that he misstated his income. During a court case, the burden of proof is on the IRS if it used a reconstruction of records solely to estimate Ken's liability.

Understanding Tax Law and the Courts

The Internal Revenue Code (IRC) is the main body of tax law of the United States. It is published as "Title 26" of the United States Code.

Other tax law is promulgated by individual states, cities, and municipalities. The IRS enrolled agent exam deals only with federal tax laws and not with the laws of any individual state or municipality.

Tax law is decided by all three branches of our federal government. The legislative branch (Congress) is responsible for the Internal Revenue Code and Congressional committee reports. The executive branch (the president) is responsible for income tax regulations, revenue rulings, and revenue procedures. The judicial branch (the courts) is responsible for court decisions.

Tax law is *primarily* decided by Congress, and it changes every year. Laws passed by Congress are the main source of IRC tax law.

The IRS is a federal agency that has the responsibility of *enforcing* tax law. It is the "collection arm" for the U.S. Treasury, which is responsible for paying various government expenses. The Department of the Treasury issues administrative pronouncements, including Treasury regulations, which interpret and illustrate the rules contained in the Internal Revenue Code.

In its role of administering the tax laws enacted by Congress, the IRS takes the specifics of these laws and translates them into the detailed regulations, rules, and procedures of the IRC.

Often, taxpayers and tax practitioners will disagree with the IRS's interpretation of the IRC. In these cases, it is up to the courts to determine Congress's intent or the constitutionality of the tax law or IRS position that is being challenged. There are many instances in which tax laws are either disputed or overturned. Court decisions then serve as guidance for future tax decisions.

The enrolled agent exam is based almost entirely on IRS publications, and exam candidates will not be tested on court cases unless the law has already made its way into an IRS publication. Likewise, if there is current pending tax law or legislation, the exam candidate will not be tested on any pending tax law; the exam will always be based on tax law from a prior year. However, EA candidates must understand the basics of tax law, the court system, and how it relates to the taxpayer.

The Court System

If a taxpayer does not agree with IRS appeals, the taxpayer may go to court. As mentioned earlier, a taxpayer may challenge the IRS in any of three courts: the U.S. Tax Court, the U.S. Court of Federal Claims, or the U.S. District Court.

Court precedent usually decides where the litigation should begin. The court system, for tax purposes, is organized as follows:

1. The U.S. Tax Court
2. District courts
3. Court of Federal Claims
4. Appellate courts
5. U.S. Supreme Court

If a taxpayer wishes to challenge the IRS in a U.S. district court (or any other court besides the U.S. Tax Court), he must pay the contested tax deficiency *first*. The taxpayer must then petition the court for a refund, essentially "suing the IRS" to have the disputed liability returned.

Example: The IRS chooses Peg's tax return for examination, which issues a deficiency of $45,000. Peg disagrees with the examiner's findings and does not wish to go through IRS appeals. Peg also does not wish to go to Tax Court. Instead, she wants to go straight to a U.S. District Court. In order to do so, she must first pay the contested liability and then sue the IRS for a refund.

If either party loses at the trial court level, the court's decision may be appealed to a higher court. In most cases, the burden of proof lies with the IRS during court proceedings, assuming the taxpayer has complied with all of the issues listed below:

*   Adhered to IRS substantiation requirements
*   Maintained adequate records

- Cooperated with reasonable requests for information from the IRS
- Introduced credible evidence relating to the issue
- Have tax liability of $7 million or less if the taxpayer is a trust, corporation, or partnership

The Tax Court is a federal court where taxpayers may choose to contest their tax deficiencies without having to pay the disputed amount first. The court issues both regular and memorandum decisions.

"Memorandum decisions" are court cases where the U.S. Tax Court has previously ruled on identical or similar issues. A "regular decision" is when the Tax Court rules on an issue for the first time.

The Tax Court has jurisdiction over the following **tax disputes** only:

1. Notices of deficiency
2. Review of the failure to abate interest
3. Notices of transferee liability
4. Adjustment of partnership items
5. Administrative costs
6. Worker classification (employee versus independent contractor)
7. Review of certain collection actions

The Tax Court has jurisdiction over the following **types of tax** only:

1. Income tax
2. Estate tax and gift tax
3. Certain excise taxes
4. Re-determine transferee liability
5. Worker classification
6. Relief from joint and several liability on a joint return
7. Whistleblower awards

This list is not exhaustive.

EAs and CPAs who want to represent taxpayers in Tax Court must be admitted to practice before Tax Court by first passing a separate exam specific to this purpose. Only licensed attorneys are not required to take the Tax Court exam before practicing before the court. However, any individual taxpayer may represent himself before the U.S. Tax Court.

Small Tax Case Procedure

Tax law provides for small tax case procedures (also known as S-case procedures) for resolving disputes between taxpayers and the IRS. A taxpayer may elect the small tax case procedure for cases involving up to $50,000 in deficiency per year, including penalties and other additions to tax, but *excluding* interest. Most taxpayers who elect the small tax case procedure are *"pro se"* litigants, which means that the taxpayer has chosen to represent himself before the court.

The taxpayer and the Tax Court must both agree to proceed with the small case procedure. Generally, the Tax Court will agree with the taxpayer's request if the taxpayer otherwise qualifies.

Small tax cases are handled under simpler, less formal procedures than regular cases. Often, decisions are handed down quicker than in other courts.

However, the Tax Court's decision in a small tax case CANNOT be appealed by the taxpayer. The decision is final (the IRS is not allowed to appeal either, if it loses the case.) In contrast, the taxpayer and the IRS can appeal a decision in a regular, non-S case to a U.S. Court of Appeals.

Dollar limits for the Tax Court Small Case Division vary:

- For a "Notice of Deficiency": $50,000 is the maximum amount, including penalties and interest, for any year before the court.
- For a "Notice of Determination": $50,000 is the maximum amount for all the years combined.
- For a "Notice of Deficiency" related to a request for relief from joint and several liability: $50,000 is the maximum amount of spousal relief for all the years combined.
- For an "IRS Notice of Determination of Worker Classification": The amount in the dispute cannot exceed $50,000 for any calendar quarter.

A decision entered in a small tax case is not treated as precedent for any other case and a decision is not typically published.

Since the taxpayer cannot appeal a decision from the Small Tax Case division, he must consider if using the S-case procedure is worth the risk. A taxpayer who uses the regular U.S. Tax Court retains the right to appeal his case to a higher court. The IRS cannot attempt to influence a taxpayer to waive his rights to sue the

United States or a government officer or employee for any action taken in connection with the tax laws.

IRS Acquiescence

The IRS may choose whether or not to acquiesce to a court decision. This means that the IRS may choose to ignore the decision of the court and continue with its regular policies regarding the litigated issue. The IRS is not bound to change its regulations due to a loss in court. The only exception to this rule is the U.S. Supreme Court, whose decisions the IRS is obligated to follow.

The IRS publishes its acquiescence and non-acquiescence first in the Internal Revenue Bulletin and then in the Cumulative Bulletin. The Internal Revenue Bulletin (IRB) is the authoritative publication for announcing official rulings and procedures of the IRS and for publishing Treasury decisions, executive orders, tax conventions, legislation, and court decisions.

The IRS does not announce acquiescence or non-acquiescence in every case. Sometimes the IRS's position is withheld.

Recovering Litigation or Administrative Costs

If the court agrees with the taxpayer on most issues in the case and finds that the IRS's position is unjustified, the taxpayer may be able to recover administrative and litigation costs. These are the expenses that a taxpayer incurs to defend his position to the IRS or the courts.

The taxpayer may be able to recover reasonable litigation or administrative costs if all of the following conditions apply:

- The taxpayer is the prevailing party.
- The taxpayer has exhausted all administrative remedies within the IRS.
- The taxpayer's "net worth" is below a certain limit.
- The taxpayer does not unreasonably delay any IRS proceeding.

The taxpayer will not be treated as the "prevailing party" if the IRS establishes that its position was substantially justified. The position of the IRS is not considered "substantially justified" if either of the following applies:

- The IRS did not follow its applicable published guidance (such as regulations, revenue rulings, notices, announcements, private letter rulings, technical advice memoranda, and determination letters issued to the tax-payer) in the proceeding. This presumption can be overcome by evidence.

- The IRS has lost in courts of appeal for other circuits on substantially similar issues.

The court will generally decide who the "prevailing party" is.

Net Worth Requirements for Recovering Litigation Costs

In order to request the recovery of litigation costs from the IRS, the taxpayer must meet certain net worth requirements:

- For individuals, net worth cannot exceed $2 million as of the filing date of the petition for review. For this purpose, individuals filing a joint return are treated as separate individuals.
- For estates, net worth cannot exceed $2 million as of the date of the decedent's death.
- For charities and certain cooperatives, the entity cannot have more than 500 employees as of the filing date of the petition for review.
- For all other taxpayers, net worth cannot exceed $7 million and the entity must not have more than 500 employees as of the filing date of the petition for review.

The taxpayer may apply for administrative costs within 90 days of the date of the mailing of the final decision of the IRS Office of Appeals regarding the tax, interest, or penalty.

Delay Tactics are Not Permitted in the Tax Court

If a taxpayer unreasonably fails to pursue the internal IRS's appeals system, if the case is filed primarily to cause a delay, or if the taxpayer's position is frivolous, the Tax Court may impose a penalty of up to $25,000.[59] "Frivolous positions" include those that contend that:

- The income tax is not valid,
- Payment of tax is voluntary,
- A person or a type of income is not subject to tax,

---

[59] The IRS makes public the names and cases of taxpayers who have been assessed these Section 6673 penalties by the Tax Court. The cases are published on the IRS website as well as in the Tax Court Historical Opinion area.

- Or espouse other arguments that the courts have previously rejected as baseless.

The Tax Court may also impose sanctions of up to $25,000 on those who misuse their right to a court review of IRS collection procedures merely to stall their tax payments.

This rule is basically targeted at taxpayers who do not have a legitimate complaint and are instead using the Tax Court simply to delay collection action in their case.

Unit 9: Questions

1. With an IRS appeal, which of the following statements is correct?

A. An appeal does not abate the interest, which continues to accrue.
B. A taxpayer must pay the disputed tax before filing an appeal with the IRS.
C. The IRS is prohibited from filing a federal tax lien if the taxpayer is outside the U.S.
D. Taxpayers who do not agree to the IRS changes may not appeal to the U.S. Tax Court.

The answer is A. An IRS appeal does not abate the interest, which continues to accrue until the balance of the debt is paid, or until the taxpayer wins his appeal and he is granted a no-change audit. A no-change audit means the IRS has accepted the tax return as it was filed. ###

2. The Statutory Notice of Deficiency is also known as:

A. A 30-day letter because the taxpayer generally has 30 days from the date of the letter to file a petition with the Tax Court.
B. A 90-day letter because the taxpayer generally has 90 days from the date of the letter to file a petition with the Tax Court.
C. An Information Document Request because the taxpayer is asked for information to support his position regarding liability for tax.
D. A federal tax lien.

The answer is B. The Statutory Notice of Deficiency, or 90-day letter, gives the taxpayer 90 days to file a petition in the U.S. Tax Court challenging the proposed deficiency. ###

3. Abigail received a Statutory Notice of Deficiency from the IRS. Abigail's permanent address is in Scotland. How many days does she have to respond and file a petition with the Tax Court?

A. 30 days.
B. 90 days.
C. 150 days.
D. 365 days.

The answer is C. The taxpayer normally has 90 days to respond to a Notice of Deficiency. However, a taxpayer is granted 150 days if the notice is addressed to a taxpayer outside the United States. ###

4. The IRS selects Aaron's return for examination. After the audit is concluded, he disputes the findings. He wants to go to appeals, but his tax return was prepared by an unenrolled practitioner. Aaron does not wish to be present during the appeals process. What are his options?

A. Aaron may only represent himself at IRS Appeals.
B. Aaron may represent himself or hire an enrolled preparer (CPA, attorney, or EA) to represent him at the appeals level.
C. Aaron may choose to forgo the appeals process and mail in his dispute.
D. Aaron may ask an IRS employee to represent him at IRS Appeals.

The answer is B. Aaron can appear before IRS Appeals by himself, or hire a qualified representative to appear on his behalf. If he wants to be represented by someone else, he must choose a person who is qualified to practice before the IRS. Only enrolled preparers (usually, attorneys, CPAs, and EAs) are allowed to represent taxpayers before an appeals hearing. ###

5. At the beginning of each examination, the IRS auditor must explain _____.

A. A taxpayer's appeal rights.
B. A taxpayer's right to a fair trial.
C. A taxpayer's right to remain silent.
D. A taxpayer's right to confidentiality.

The answer is A. At the beginning of each examination, the IRS auditor must explain a taxpayer's appeal rights. ###

6. Karl had his 2010 and 2011 income tax returns examined, resulting in adjustments. He has administratively appealed the adjustments through the IRS appeals process. Some of them were sustained, resulting in an income tax deficiency in the amount of $25,000 for 2010 and $27,000 for 2011. Karl now wants to appeal his case to the U.S. Tax Court. He will handle the case himself since he cannot afford a lawyer or other representative. Which of the following is true?

A. Karl has forfeited his rights to the small tax case procedure by going to appeals first.
B. Karl is entitled to invoke the small tax case procedure.
C. Karl is not entitled to the small tax case procedure because his disputed amount exceeds $50,000.
D. Karl must appeal to the U.S. District Court first.

The answer is B. A taxpayer may elect the small tax case procedure (also known as S case procedure) for cases involving up to $50,000 in deficiency **per year**, including penalties and other additions to tax, but excluding interest. Trials in small tax cases generally are less formal and result in a speedier disposition. However, small tax court cases may not be appealed. Decisions are final for both the taxpayer and the IRS. ###

7. Alyssa vehemently disagrees with the IRS examiner regarding her income tax case. Her appeal rights are explained to her, and she decides to go to Tax Court. Which of the following is true?

A. Alyssa must receive a Notice of Deficiency before she can go to Tax Court.
B. Alyssa must wait for the IRS examiner to permanently close her audit case.
C. Alyssa must request a collection due process hearing before going to Tax Court.
D. Alyssa cannot go to Tax Court unless she agrees with the auditor's findings.

The answer is A. A Notice of Deficiency (90-day letter) must be issued before a taxpayer can go to Tax Court. Once the taxpayer receives the Notice of Deficiency, she then has 90 days to respond and file a petition with the court. ###

8. What branch of government decides tax law?

A. Tax law is written by the Treasury Department.
B. Tax law is primarily written by the President.
C. Tax law is primarily decided by Congress.
D. Tax law is written by the Internal Revenue Service.

The answer is C. Tax law is primarily decided by Congress, and it changes every year. Laws passed by Congress are the main source of Internal Revenue Code tax law. ###

9. Morgan wants her income tax case to be handled under the Tax Court's small tax case procedure. All of the following statements regarding the small tax case procedure are correct except:

A. In tax disputes involving $50,000 or less, taxpayers may choose to use the IRS small tax case procedure.
B. The disputed amount must be paid before going to Tax Court.
C. The Tax Court must approve the request that the case be handled under the small tax case procedure.
D. The decision is final and cannot be appealed.

The answer is B. The disputed amount does not have to be paid before going to Tax Court. In tax disputes involving $50,000 or less, taxpayers may choose to use the IRS small tax case procedure, and the Tax Court must approve the request. The decision in a small tax case procedure is final and cannot be appealed. ###

10. Danielle owes a substantial sum to the IRS. She files a petition with the U.S. Tax Court. Her case is later determined to be frivolous, wholly without merit, and merely to cause delay. What is the potential repercussion of Danielle's actions?

A. The Tax Court may impose a penalty of up to $10,000.
B. The Tax Court may impose a penalty of up to $25,000.
C. The Tax Court may impose a penalty of up to $50,000.
D. The Tax Court may impose a penalty of up to $25,000 and one year in prison.

The answer is B. If a taxpayer unreasonably fails to pursue the internal IRS appeals system, if the case is filed primarily to cause a delay, or if the taxpayer's position is frivolous, the Tax Court may impose a penalty of up to $25,000. ###

11. The Commissioner of the IRS has decided to publicly non-acquiesce to a court decision. Where will this decision be published?

A. The Internal Revenue Bulletin.
B. The New York Times.
C. Only on the IRS website.
D. The Tax Court website.

The answer is A. The IRS publishes its acquiescence and non-acquiescence first in the Internal Revenue Bulletin and then in the Cumulative Bulletin. The IRS does not announce acquiescence or non-acquiescence in every case. ###

12. If a taxpayer wishes to challenge the IRS in a district court, the taxpayer must _____:

A. Pay the contested liability first, and then sue the Department of Treasury for a refund.
B. Pay the contested liability first, and then sue the IRS for a refund.
C. Pay a retainer to the IRS for a refund.
D. Go first to the U.S. Tax Court before appealing to the U.S. District Court.

The answer is B. In order to appeal in a district court, the taxpayer must first pay the contested liability and then sue the IRS for a refund. If either party loses at the trial court level, the court's decision may be appealed to a higher court. ###

13. Which of the following statements is true regarding IRS acquiescence?

A. The IRS may choose whether or not to acquiesce to any court decision.
B. The IRS must change its regulations due to a loss in court.
C. The IRS will announce acquiescence or non-acquiescence in every case.
D. The IRS is bound to follow U.S. Supreme Court decisions.

The answer is D. The IRS may choose whether or not to acquiesce to a court decision. The only exception to this rule is the U.S. Supreme Court, whose decisions the IRS is obligated to follow. The IRS is not bound to change its regulations due to a loss in court. The IRS does not announce acquiescence or non-acquiescence in every case. Sometimes the IRS's position is withheld. ###

14. Kevin and Javier are partners in a body shop business. Both had their individual returns examined and both disagreed with the IRS. Kevin decided to take his case to IRS Appeals. After the conference, he and the IRS still disagreed. Javier decided to bypass IRS Appeals altogether and go directly to court. Which of the following is true?

A. Both Kevin and Javier can take their cases to the following courts: United States Tax Court, the United States Court of Federal Claims, or the United States District Court.
B. Only Kevin may petition the U.S. Tax Court, because he went through the IRS appeals process first.
C. Neither may petition the U.S. Tax Court, because they chose to use IRS Appeals first.
D. None of the above.

The answer is A. Both Kevin and Javier can take their cases to court. A taxpayer is not required to use the IRS appeals process. If a taxpayer and the IRS still disagree after an appeals conference or a taxpayer decides to bypass the IRS appeals system, the case may be taken to the U.S. Tax Court, the U.S. Court of Federal Claims, or a U.S. district court. ###

15. Which tax professional is allowed to practice before the U.S. Tax Court without first passing a qualifying test?

A. Enrolled agent.
B. CPA.
C. Attorney.
D. Both B and C.

The answer is C. Only licensed attorneys are allowed to practice before the U.S. Tax Court without passing a qualifying test. EAs and CPAs must first take a separate exam that gives them the right to practice before the Tax Court. ###

16. Which statement is correct regarding the IRS appeals process?

A. No written statement is required for tax deficiencies of $10,000 or less.
B. If the disputed tax deficiency is more than $10,000, a taxpayer must file a formal written protest.
C. The local IRS Appeals office and local IRS district offices are the same entities.
D. The 30-day letter that is sent to a taxpayer details the date and location of an upcoming audit, and includes an agreement or waiver form.

The answer is B. In cases in which the taxpayer owes more than $10,000, a taxpayer must file a formal written protest. Only in cases of $2,500 or less is no written statement required, though the taxpayer is required to contact the IRS to initiate an appeal. When a taxpayer owes more than $2,500 and less than $10,000, he must include a brief statement of disputed tax. The IRS Appeals office is a separate entity from local IRS district offices. The 30-day letter is sent to a taxpayer after an audit is concluded and includes an agreement or waiver form and a notice explaining appeal rights. ###

Unit 10: IRS E-File and IRS Payments

More Reading:

Publication 3112, *IRS e-file Application and Participation*

Publication 1345, *Handbook for Authorized IRS e-file Providers*

Publication 4169, *Tax Professional Guide to Electronic Federal Tax Payment System*

Publication 4453, *IRS e-file for Charities and Nonprofits*

Publication 3611, *Easy Ways to Pay Electronically*

The IRS e-file program allows taxpayers to transmit their returns electronically. Last year more than 80% of American taxpayers filed electronically. According to the IRS, the processing of e-file returns is not only quicker but also more accurate than the processing of paper returns. However, as with a paper return, the taxpayer is responsible for making sure the tax return contains accurate information and is filed on time.[60]

The E-File Mandate

A law requiring most tax preparers to e-file income tax returns went into effect in 2011.[61] The mandate covers returns for individuals, trusts, and estates (fiduciary returns, Form 1041).

Any tax return preparer who anticipates preparing and filing 11 or more Forms 1040, 1040A, 1040EZ, and 1041 during a calendar year must use IRS e-file (with limited exceptions explained later.) Those who are subject to the e-file requirement are referred to as "specified tax return preparers."

The rules require tax firms to compute the number of returns *in aggregate* that they reasonably expect to file as a firm. If that number is 11 or more for the calendar year, then all members of the firm must e-file the returns they prepare and file. This is true even if, on an individual basis, a member prepares and files fewer than the threshold.

*Exceptions: Financial institutions and fiduciaries that file Forms 1041 as *a trustee or fiduciary* are not required to e-file and are not subject to the mandate. [62] The e-file mandate also does not apply to payroll tax returns.

---

[60]The IRS e-file rules and requirements are included in Revenue Procedure 2007-40, throughout Publication 3112, and in other IRS e-file publications and notices on the IRS website.

[61] Internal Revenue Bulletin: 2011-17, April 25, 2011, T.D. 9518, *Specified Tax Return Preparers Required to File Individual Income Tax Returns Using Magnetic Media.*

Example: Caroline is an EA who works for a CPA firm. She also has a small side business doing tax returns from her home. For the coming tax year, Caroline expects to prepare and file five Forms 1041 (for estates and trusts) while working for the CPA firm. She also expects to prepare and file ten Form 1040 tax returns individually as a self-employed preparer. Since she expects to file 11 or more forms, Caroline is required to e-file tax returns. The number of returns must be considered *in aggregate.*

Taxpayers may independently choose to file on paper. Even if a practitioner has prepared the return, a taxpayer may mail the return himself, if he includes a hand-signed and dated statement documenting his choice to file on paper.

A tax preparer may also request a hardship waiver from the IRS to be exempt from e-filing. IRS says it will grant waivers only in rare cases and usually not for more than one calendar year. It will deny waivers based solely on the fact a preparer doesn't have a computer or appropriate software, or prefers simply not to e-file.

Some returns are impossible to e-file for various reasons and are therefore exempt from the e-file requirement. The IRS also may grant administrative exemptions when technology issues prevent specified preparers from filing returns electronically. Whatever the reason for paper filing, preparers generally are required to attach Form 8948, *Preparer Explanation for Not Filing Electronically*, to clients' paper returns.

Authorized IRS E-File Provider

An authorized IRS e-file provider is a business authorized by the IRS to participate in IRS e-file. The business may be a sole proprietorship, partnership, or corporation. The applicant must identify its principals and at least one responsible official on its IRS e-file application. Each individual who is a principal or responsible official must:

- Be a United States citizen or a legal U.S. alien lawfully admitted for permanent residence;
- Be at least 21 years of age as of the date of application; and

---

[62]Fiduciaries, as described by Section 7701(a)(36)(B)(iii) of the Internal Revenue Code, that file returns are not considered tax return preparers and are therefore not covered by the e-file requirement.

- Meet applicable state and local licensing and/or bonding requirements for the preparation and collection of tax returns.

Applying to the E-File Program

To begin e-filing tax returns, a practitioner must first apply and be accepted as an authorized IRS e-file provider. There is no fee to apply to the IRS, and the process takes up to 45 days.

When a business is accepted to participate in IRS e-file, it is assigned an Electronic Filing Identification Number (EFIN), which is required to file electronically. EFINs are issued on a firm basis, with all preparers in a firm covered by the same number. So, for example, a tax preparation business that has ten employee-preparers in one location would all file using the same EFIN. Each preparer would then use his own PTIN on the returns that he individually prepares.

E-File Suitability Check

The IRS will conduct a suitability check on the applicant and on all principals and responsible officials listed on an application to determine their suitability to be authorized e-file providers. Suitability checks may include the following:

- A criminal background check
- A credit history check
- A tax compliance check to ensure that the applicant's personal returns are filed and paid
- A check for prior noncompliance with IRS e-file requirements

Denial to Participate in IRS E-File

An applicant may be denied participation in IRS e-file for a variety of reasons that includes but is not limited to:

- Conviction of any criminal offense under the revenue laws of the United States or of a state or other political subdivision
- Failure to timely file returns
- Failure to timely pay any federal, state, or local tax liability
- Assessment of penalties
- Suspension/disbarment from practice before the IRS or before a state or local tax agency

- Disreputable conduct or other facts that may adversely impact IRS e-file
- Misrepresentation on an IRS e-file application
- Unethical practices in return preparation
- Failure to sign the preparer's area of the tax return
- Stockpiling returns prior to official acceptance to participate in IRS e-file
- Knowingly and directly or indirectly employing or accepting assistance from any firm, organization, or individual denied participation in IRS e-file, or suspended or expelled from participating in IRS e-file

Businesses That Are Required to E-File

Certain corporations, partnerships, and tax-exempt organizations are required to e-file. Some other businesses are also required to e-file their tax returns. The IRS has long mandated this rule in order to improve accuracy and processing of complicated returns.

Partnerships with more than 100 partners are required to file electronically. This means that a partnership must file Form 1065 and the multiple Schedules K-1 electronically. Partnerships with 100 or fewer partners (Schedules K-1) may voluntarily file their returns electronically, but they are not required to e-file.

Large and midsized corporate taxpayers, including tax-exempt organizations with $10 million or more in assets that file at least 250 returns (information returns and others, such as Form 1099 and Form W-2), are required to e-file.

The e-file application must be current and must list all the form types (1120, 1065, 990, etc.) that the practitioner will transmit to the IRS. If the practitioner does not list a certain form on his application and later attempts to transmit that form, he will receive a rejection for return type.

> **Example:** Karen is an EA. When she first applied to be an e-file provider, she only prepared individual returns. In tax year 2012, she wishes to prepare a partnership return. However, Karen forgets to update her e-file application. When she submits the partnership return online, it is rejected. Karen will have to update her e-file application in order to submit partnership returns electronically.

Resubmission of Rejected Tax Returns

All prescribed due dates for filing paper income tax returns also apply to electronic returns. If the IRS rejects an e-filed return and the preparer cannot rectify the reason for the rejection, the preparer must inform the taxpayer of the rejection within 24 hours. The preparer must provide the taxpayer with the IRS reject codes accompanied by an explanation.

If the taxpayer chooses not to have the electronic portion of the return corrected and transmitted to the IRS, or if the IRS cannot accept the return for processing, the taxpayer must file a paper return. In order to timely file the return, the taxpayer must file the paper return by the later of:

- The due date of the return; or
- Ten calendar days after the date the IRS gives notification that it rejected the e-filed return. This is called the "Ten-day Transmission Perfection Period," and it is additional time that the IRS gives a preparer and taxpayer to correct and resubmit a tax return without a late filing penalty.

The transmission perfection period is not an extension of time to file; it is additional time to correct errors in the electronic file.

> **Example:** Russ is an EA who e-files a tax return for his client, Paravi. The e-filed return is transmitted on April 15, 2013. The next day, Russ receives a rejection notification from the IRS regarding her tax return. Russ properly notifies Paravi of the rejection within 24 hours. The issue cannot be corrected, so she must file a paper return. Russ gives Paravi a copy of the paper return on April 17, 2013, along with an attached statement explaining the rejection. The tax return will be considered filed timely, because the paper return was filed within ten days of the rejection and the original e-filed return was attempted in a timely manner.

After an e-file rejection, a taxpayer may want to file on paper. To ensure that the paper return is identified as a rejected electronic return and the taxpayer is given credit for timely filing, the following information must be included:

- An explanation of why the paper return is being filed after the due date
- A copy of the rejection notification
- A brief history of actions taken to correct the electronic return

The taxpayer should write in red at the top of the first page of the paper return:

The date should be the date of the first e-file rejection. The paper return must be signed by the taxpayer. The PIN that was used on the electronically-filed return that was rejected may not be used as the signature on the paper return.

It is important to note that the Ten-day Transmission Perfection Period does not apply to payments. If an e-file submission is rejected, a return can be corrected within ten days and not be subject to a late filing penalty. When a return is rejected on the due date, it is recommended that an electronic payment not be transmitted with the return, because the payment must still be submitted or post-marked by the due date.

Types of E-File Providers

There are many types of e-file providers. An e-file provider is not necessarily a tax preparer. Authorized IRS e-file providers can also be firms that develop tax software, transmit electronic returns to the IRS, and provide services to a multitude of taxpayer clients.

The roles and responsibilities of e-file providers vary according to a firm's activities. Once a firm applies for acceptance into the IRS e-file program, it selects its "provider option" at that time. Some providers may have more than one e-file activity. For example, an e-file transmitter may also be a software developer.

ERO Responsibilities

An electronic return originator (ERO) originates the electronic submission of tax returns to the IRS. An ERO is the person that the client entrusts with tax information for the purpose of filing income tax returns electronically in the IRS e-file program.

Although an ERO may engage in tax return preparation, and many of them do, tax preparation is a separate and distinct activity from the electronic submission of tax returns to the IRS. An ERO submits a tax return only after the taxpayer has authorized the e-file transmission. The return must be either:

- Prepared by the ERO; or
- Collected from a taxpayer who has self-prepared his own return and is asking the ERO to e-file it for him.

> **Example:** Patrick is an EA who uses Ultra TaxPro software to prepare returns. Once he has completed a tax return, he gives a copy to the client, who then gives signature authorization to e-file the return. Patrick transmits the return to Ultra TaxPro, which is an authorized transmitter. Ultra TaxPro then transmits the return to the IRS. Most tax practitioners use this method; all the major tax preparation software companies have e-file transmission options.

In originating the electronic submission of a return, the ERO is required to:

- Timely submit returns.
- Provide copies to taxpayers.
- Retain records and make records available to the IRS.
- Accept returns only from taxpayers and authorized IRS e-file providers, and work with the taxpayer and/or the transmitter to correct a rejected return.
- Enter the preparer's identifying information (name, address, and PTIN).
- Be diligent in recognizing fraud and abuse, reporting it to the IRS, and preventing it when possible.
- Cooperate with IRS investigations by making documents available to the IRS upon request.

To become an ERO, an applicant must apply and be accepted into the program, and then receive an EFIN. All EROs must be fingerprinted.

Permissible Disclosures

Disclosure of client information between e-file providers is permissible, so long as the disclosures are for the preparation and transmission of the tax return. For example, an ERO may relay tax return information to a transmitter for the purpose of transmitting the forms to the IRS.

However, if tax return information is disclosed or used in any other way, a provider may be subject to IRS penalties or the civil penalties in Internal Revenue Code (IRC) §6713 for unauthorized disclosure or use of tax return information.

Electronic Signature Requirements

As with any income tax return submitted to the IRS, the taxpayer and preparer must both sign the tax return. If an electronic return does not have an appropriate signature, it will be rejected.

All e-file individual returns submitted to the IRS by tax practitioners must be electronically signed using a PIN. These requirements also apply to volunteers at VITA and TCE sites who provide free tax assistance and e-filing.

- **The Self-Select PIN** allows taxpayers to electronically sign their e-filed return by using a five-digit PIN to act as their signature. The IRS uses the taxpayer's prior year adjusted gross income or prior year PIN to validate the taxpayer's signature. This signature method is available if the taxpayer SELECTS and ENTERS his own PIN on the electronically filed return.

- **The Practitioner PIN** is another signature method for taxpayers who use an ERO. The ERO asks the taxpayer to choose a five-digit, self-selected PIN as his electronic signature. The ERO must then complete Form 8879, *IRS e-file Signature Authorization*, and include the *taxpayer's* self-selected PIN and his own *practitioner* PIN. The Practitioner PIN is an 11-digit number that includes the ERO's EFIN plus five other digits that he chooses. The ERO should use the same practitioner PIN for the entire tax year.

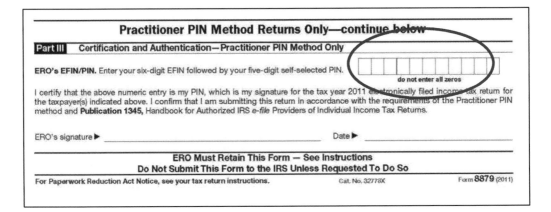

The ERO must sign and complete the requested information in the area provided: *"Declaration of Electronic Return Originator [ERO]."* An ERO may authorize employees to sign for him, but the ERO is ultimately responsible for all electronically-filed returns by its firm. If the return was prepared for a fee, the ERO must also sign the jurat.[63] EROs may sign this form by rubber stamp, mechanical device (such as signature pen), or computer software program.

---

[63]Jurat: An affidavit in which the taxpayer and/or preparer attests to the truth of the information contained in the return and attached return information.

The ERO must retain copies of Forms 8879 for three years from the return due date or the IRS received date, whichever is later. EROs must not send Forms 8879 to the IRS unless requested to do so.

E-filed returns signed by a representative with power of attorney may be submitted to the IRS using Form 8453.[64] Form 2848, *Power of Attorney and Declaration of Representative,* is then submitted as an attachment. An e-filed return signed by an agent must have a power of attorney attached to Form 8453 that *specifically authorizes* the agent to sign the return.

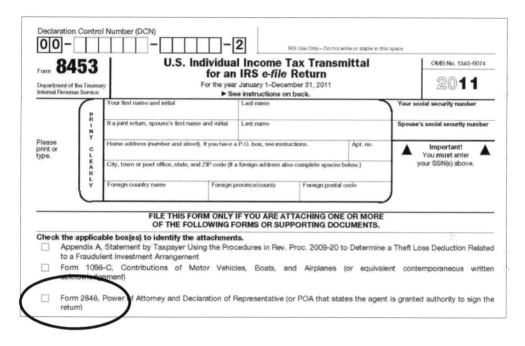

After Signing the Return

After the taxpayer signs the return, the ERO transmits the return to the IRS or to a third-party transmitter who then forwards the entire electronic record to the IRS for processing. Once received at the IRS, the return is automatically checked for errors. If it cannot be processed, it is sent back to the originating transmitter (usually the preparer) to clarify any necessary information.

After correction, the transmitter retransmits the return to the IRS. Within 48 hours of electronically sending the return, the IRS sends an acknowledgment to the transmitter stating the return is accepted for processing. This is called an "elec-

---

[64]See Publication 17 for updated procedures for attaching a power of attorney to electronically filed returns.

tronic postmark" and it is the taxpayer's proof of filing and assurance that the IRS has the return.

A tax preparer must retain a record of each electronic postmark until the end of the calendar year and provide the record to the IRS upon request. Most tax software packages automatically retain a record of the return transmission report and electronic postmark.

EROs Who Make Changes to a Return

An ERO who originates returns that he has not prepared but only collected becomes an "income tax return preparer" when he makes "substantive changes" to the tax return. A "non-substantive change" is a correction limited to a transposition error, misplaced entry, spelling error, or arithmetic correction. The IRS considers all other changes "substantive," and the ERO *becomes* a tax return preparer when he makes these changes.

As such, the ERO may be required to sign the return as the preparer.

> **Example:** Diana is an ERO. A taxpayer brings a self-prepared tax return for Diana to e-file. She notices gross errors on the tax return and talks with the client about the mistakes. The taxpayer agrees to correct the return, and Diana makes the necessary adjustments, in return for a small fee. Diana is now required to sign the return as a preparer.

Signature forms must be retained by the e-file provider for three years from the due date of the return, extended due date, or the IRS received date, whichever is later. Providers must make all these records available to the IRS upon request.

Providers may electronically image (scan) and store all paper records they are required to retain for IRS e-file. This includes signed documents as well as any supporting documents not included in the electronic record.

Providing a Copy of an E-filed Return to the Taxpayer

An ERO is required to submit an e-filed return to the IRS that is *identical* to the return provided to the taxpayer. The ERO is also required to provide a complete copy of the return to the taxpayer.

The copy given to the taxpayer may be in any media acceptable to both the taxpayer and the provider (for example, the taxpayer may request a scanned copy on disk or a paper copy.) The copy that is given to the taxpayer is not required to be signed by the preparer (only the copy that is filed with the IRS, whether electronic or on a paper return, requires a preparer's signature).

The taxpayer should retain this information for a minimum of three years from the due date of the tax return, extended due date, or the date the return was filed, whichever is later. This corresponds to the statute of limitations for that tax period.

E-File Advertising Standards

"IRS e-file" is a brand name, but acceptance to the IRS e-file program does not imply an endorsement by the IRS. A practitioner must not use improper or misleading advertising in relation to IRS e-file, including promising a time frame for refunds and Refund Anticipation Loans (RALs). If a practitioner advertises an RAL or other financial product, he and the financial institution must clearly describe the RAL as a loan, not as a refund. The advertisement on an RAL or other financial product must be easy to identify and in easily readable print.

Practitioners may not use the regular IRS logo (the eagle symbol) or IRS insignia in their advertising, or imply any type of relationship with the IRS. A practitioner may, however, use the IRS *e-file* logo.

A preparer may not combine the e-file logo with the IRS eagle symbol, the word "federal," or with other words or symbols that might suggest a special relationship with the IRS. A preparer's advertising materials must not carry the FMS, IRS, or any other Treasury seals.

The IRS e-file logo, which preparers may use

If an e-file provider uses radio, television, Internet, signage, or other methods of advertising, the practitioner must keep a copy and provide it to the IRS upon request. Practitioners must retain copies of any advertising until the end of the calendar year following the last transmission or use.

A practitioner may not advertise that individual income tax returns may be e-filed without using Forms W-2. In other words, a firm may not advertise that it can file a tax return using only "pay stubs" or "earnings statements."

E-file Revocations and Sanctions

The IRS may revoke e-file privileges if a firm is either:

- Prohibited or disbarred from filing returns by a court order, or
- Prohibited from filing returns by any federal or state legal action that forbids participation in e-file.

An authorized IRS e-file provider is not entitled to an administrative review hearing if e-file privileges are revoked because of a court injunction. If the injunction or other legal action expires or is later reversed, only *then* may the practitioner reapply to participate in IRS e-file.

Example: Steve was a CPA who was convicted of felony embezzlement. He was also disbarred and stripped of his license by his state accountancy board. The IRS revoked his e-file privileges without prior notice.

The IRS may also choose to sanction any practitioner that fails to comply with any e-file regulation. Before sanctioning, the IRS may issue a warning letter that describes specific corrective action the provider must take. The IRS may also sanction a provider without issuance of a warning letter.

Sanctions may include a written reprimand, suspension, or permanent expulsion from IRS e-file. The IRS categorizes the seriousness of infractions as Level One, Level Two, and Level Three. Level One is the least serious, Level Two is moderately serious, and Level Three is the most serious. For minor violations, the IRS will usually issue a written warning to the practitioner.

Suspensions make providers ineligible to participate in IRS e-file for a period of either one or two years from the effective date of the sanction. If a principal or responsible official is suspended or expelled from participation in IRS e-file, every entity listed on the firm's e-file application may also be expelled.

The IRS may list in the Internal Revenue Bulletin, newsletters, or other media the name and owner of any entity suspended or expelled from participation in IRS e- file and the effective date of the IRS action.

Practitioners who are denied or expelled from participation in IRS e-file usually have the right to an administrative review. Failure to respond within 30 days of the date of any denial or sanction letter irrevocably terminates the practitioner's right to an administrative review or appeal.

In order to appeal, practitioners must mail a written response within 30 days addressing the IRS's reason for denial or revocation and including supporting documentation. During this administrative review process, the denial of participation remains in effect.

In certain circumstances, the IRS can immediately suspend or expel an authorized IRS e-file provider without prior notice.

Refunds and Payments on E-Filed Returns

Taxpayers have several options for refunds and payments on electronically-filed returns. The IRS has attempted to make Direct Deposit[65] and automatic payments easier in order to encourage these methods.

Taxpayers often elect the Direct Deposit option because it is the fastest way of receiving their refund. Taxpayers may:

- Apply the refund to next year's estimated tax.
- Receive the refund as a Direct Deposit.
- Receive the refund as a paper check.
- Split the refund, with a portion applied to next year's estimated tax and the remainder received as Direct Deposit or a paper check.
- Use their federal tax refund (or part of it) to purchase U.S. Series I Savings Bonds by completing Form 8888, *Allocation of Refund (Including Savings Bond Purchases)*. Taxpayers can purchase up to $5,000 in bonds for themselves or others, such as a child or grandchild.

Direct Deposit

Providers are required to accept any Direct Deposit election to any eligible financial institution designated by the taxpayer. A provider may not charge a separate fee for Direct Deposit. The provider must not alter the Direct Deposit information in the electronic record after a taxpayer has signed the tax return.

---

[65]The IRS requires tax practitioners to capitalize the words "Direct Deposit" in their advertising, so we will use the same formatting here.

Taxpayers can split their deposits in up to three different accounts. Most e-file and tax preparation software allows taxpayers to split refunds.

Refunds may be designated for Direct Deposit to qualified accounts in the taxpayer's name. Qualified accounts include savings, checking, share draft, or retirement accounts (for example, IRA or money market accounts). Direct Deposits cannot be made to credit card accounts. Qualified accounts must be in financial institutions within the United States.

The provider must advise the taxpayer that a Direct Deposit election cannot be rescinded. In addition, changes cannot be made to routing numbers of financial institutions or to the taxpayer's account numbers after the IRS has accepted the return. Providers should verify account and routing numbers each year. Taxpayers will not receive Direct Deposit of their refunds if account information is not updated to reflect current information.

Refunds that are not Direct Deposited because of errors or any other reason will be issued as paper checks, resulting in potential refund delays of up to ten weeks.

Payments on Tax Returns

Taxpayers who have their returns filed electronically have several choices when paying any taxes owed on their tax returns, as well as any estimated taxes. The following methods of payments are accepted:

1. Direct debit
2. Credit card
3. Personal check
4. Installment agreement requests

Electronic payment options include:
1. Electronic Federal Tax Payment System (EFTPS)
2. Electronic funds withdrawal
3. Federal Tax Application (same day wire transfer)

Check Payments

Balance-due payments may be made by check. Payments do not have to be mailed at the same time an electronic return is transmitted. For example, the return may be transmitted in January and the taxpayer may mail the payment on a later date. So long as the payment is mailed by the due date of the return, it will be considered timely.

On all checks or money orders, the practitioner should write the taxpayer's Taxpayer Identification Number (EIN, TIN, or SSN), the type of tax return, and the tax year to which the payment applies. The check or money order should be made payable to the "United States Treasury."

Paying an IRS Debt with an Installment Agreement

Installment agreements are arrangements in which the IRS allows taxpayers to pay liabilities over time. A taxpayer who files electronically may apply for an installment agreement once the return is processed and the tax is assessed. Taxpayers must submit Form 9465, *Request for Installment Agreement,* in order to request payments in installments. The IRS charges a one-time user fee to set up an installment agreement.

The only agreements that may be granted are those that provide for full payment of the accounts (which means that the taxpayer must agree to pay the full balance due—the taxpayer cannot use an installment agreement to negotiate a lower tax liability). During the course of the installment agreement, penalty and interest continue to accrue. No levies may be served during installment agreements.

If a taxpayer owes less than $10,000 in taxes, he will be automatically approved for an installment agreement, provided that he is up-to-date on his filing responsibilities. Installment payments are equal monthly installments, although the taxpayer may choose to pay more than the required monthly amount. Taxpayers may make their payments by check or by electronic withdrawal from their bank account.

A taxpayer with $25,000 or less in combined tax, penalties, and interest can use the IRS Online Payment Agreement and set up his installment agreement online. If a taxpayer owes more than $25,000, he may still qualify for an installment agreement, but a *Collection Information Statement*, Form 433-F, must be completed.

In accordance with law, each year the IRS mails Form CP-89, *Annual Installment Agreement Statement*, to every installment agreement taxpayer. The statement provides the dollar amount of the beginning account balance due; an itemized listing of payments; an itemized listing of penalties, interest, and other charges; and the dollar amount of the ending account balance due.

A late payment on an installment agreement will generate an automatic 30-day notice as to the cessation of the agreement, allowing the IRS to make changes to the installment agreement.

Electronic Federal Tax Payment System (EFTPS)

Balances due and estimated taxes can be paid year-round using the Electronic Federal Tax Payment System (EFTPS). Taxpayers and businesses enroll in EFTPS by using an online application.

Businesses and individuals can pay all their federal taxes using EFTPS. Individuals can pay their quarterly estimated taxes electronically using EFTPS, and they can make payments weekly, monthly, or quarterly. Both business and individual payments can be scheduled months in advance, if desired.

Businesses can schedule payments up to 120 days in advance of their tax due date. Individuals can schedule payments up to 365 days in advance of their tax due date. Domestic corporations must deposit all income tax payments by the due date of the return using EFTPS.

Refund Anticipation Loans (RALs): The Rules

A Refund Anticipation Loan (RAL) is a financial product offered by some tax offices. An RAL is not a tax refund. Instead, an RAL is a loan: money is borrowed by the taxpayer based on his anticipated tax refund.

The IRS is not involved in RALs or financial products. Tax preparers who assist taxpayers in applying for RALs or other financial products have additional responsibilities and may be sanctioned by the IRS if they fail to adhere to the following requirements. If a practitioner wants to offer RALs, he must:

- Ensure a taxpayer understands that by agreeing to an RAL or other financial product he will not receive his refund from the IRS but instead it will be sent to the financial institution.
- Advise a taxpayer that an RAL is an interest-bearing loan and not a quicker way of receiving his refund from the IRS.

- Advise a taxpayer that if a Direct Deposit is not received within the expected time frame for whatever reason, the taxpayer may be liable to the lender for additional interest and other fees.
- Advise a taxpayer of all fees and other known deductions to be paid from his refund and the remaining amount he will actually receive.
- Obtain the taxpayer's written consent to disclose information to the lending institution.
- Ensure that the return preparer does not have a "related party" conflict with the financial institution that makes an RAL agreement.
- Adhere to fee restrictions and advertising standards (explained earlier).

There are no guarantees that the IRS will deposit a taxpayer's refund within a specified time. For example, it may delay a refund due to processing problems or it may offset some or all of the refund for back taxes, child support, or other amounts that the taxpayer owes. The IRS is not liable for any loss suffered by taxpayers, practitioners, or financial institutions resulting from reduced refunds or dishonored Direct Deposits.

RAL and E-File Fee Restrictions

Providers may not base their tax preparation fees on a percentage of the refund amount or compute their fees using any figure from tax returns. A practitioner may charge an identical flat fee to all customers applying for RALs, meaning the fee cannot correspond to the amount of a refund for an individual client.

Unit 10: Questions

1. Which of the following is considered a "substantive change" to a tax return?

A. A correction in overall tax liability.
B. The correction of a spelling error.
C. The correction of a transposition error.
D. An arithmetic correction.

The answer is A. A correction that changes an individual's tax liability would be considered a "substantive change" to a return. A "non-substantive change" is a correction limited to a transposition error, misplaced entry, spelling error, or arithmetic correction. The IRS considers all other changes "substantive," and the ERO *becomes* a tax return preparer when he makes these changes.

2. Which of the following statements is true?

A. Separate fees may be charged for Direct Deposits.
B. E-file providers may not charge contingent fees based on a percentage of the refund.
B. E-file providers may not charge a fee for paper returns under any circumstances.
D. An e-file provider is not allowed to charge a fee for e-filing.

The answer is B. A practitioner may not charge a contingent fee (percentage of the refund) for preparing an original tax return. Separate fees may not be charged for Direct Deposits. However, a practitioner is allowed to charge a fee for e-filing. ###

3. An EA has a client who wishes to use Direct Deposit. Which of the following statements regarding Direct Deposit is correct?

A. An EA may not charge a fee for offering Direct Deposit.
B. An EA may advise the taxpayer to Direct Deposit to his credit card account.
C. An EA may advise the taxpayer to Direct Deposit directly into his bank account in Mexico.
D. An EA is not required to accept a Direct Deposit election from the taxpayer.

The answer is A. A practitioner cannot charge a fee for Direct Deposit. Direct Deposits cannot be made to credit card accounts. Qualified accounts must be in financial institutions within the United States. The practitioner is required to accept a Direct Deposit election by the taxpayer. ###

4. Taxpayers who have their returns filed electronically have several choices when paying any taxes owed on their tax returns, as well as any estimated taxes. Which method is not an acceptable method of paying an outstanding tax liability to the IRS?

A. Direct debit.
B. Credit card payments.
C. A U.S. Treasury bond note.
D. Installment agreements.

The answer is C. A bond note is not an acceptable method of payment. Taxpayers may pay their outstanding tax liability a variety of ways including direct debit, credit card payments, installment agreements, or payment by check. ###

5. If the IRS rejects the electronic portion of a taxpayer's return for processing and the reason for the rejection cannot be rectified with the information already provided to the ERO, what is the ERO's responsibility at that point?

A. The ERO is not legally required to notify the taxpayer.
B. The ERO must attempt to notify the taxpayer within 24 hours and provide the taxpayer with the reject code accompanied by an explanation.
C. The ERO is required to notify the taxpayer in writing within 72 hours.
D. The ERO is required to file the tax return on paper within 24 hours.

The answer is B. If the IRS rejects the electronic portion of a taxpayer's individual income tax return for processing and the reason for the rejection cannot be rectified, the ERO must take reasonable steps to inform the taxpayer of the rejection within 24 hours. The ERO must provide the taxpayer with the reject code(s) accompanied by an explanation. After receiving a rejection, the ERO is not required to file a tax return on paper. The ERO and the client should attempt to *correct* the e-file. However, if the return continues to be rejected, the taxpayer may be forced to file on paper. ###

6. All of the following statements regarding IRS installment agreements are correct except:

A. During the course of the installment agreement, penalty and interest continue to accrue.
B. A taxpayer who owes less than $10,000 in taxes will be automatically approved for an installment agreement.
C. The IRS charges a one-time user fee to set up an installment agreement.
D. IRS levies may be served during installment agreements.

The answer is D. No levies may be served during installment agreements. During the course of the installment agreement, penalty and interest continue to accrue. A taxpayer who owes less than $10,000 in taxes will automatically be approved for an installment agreement. The IRS charges a one-time user fee to set up an installment agreement. ###

7. Which logo may a practitioner use in his advertising?

A. The official IRS logo.
B. The IRS e-file logo.
C. The official seal of the U.S. Treasury.
D. The IRS eagle symbol.

The answer is B. A practitioner may use the IRS e-file logo, but may not use the IRS logo or insignia in his advertising, or imply a relationship with the IRS. A preparer may not combine the e-file logo with the IRS eagle symbol, the word "federal," or with other words or symbols that suggest a special relationship between the IRS and the logo. Advertising materials must not carry the IRS or other Treasury seals. ###

8. Mark is getting a tax refund this year. Which of the following methods is not available for Mark to receive his IRS refund?

A. Mark may apply the refund to next year's estimated tax.
B. Mark may receive the refund as a Direct Deposit to his retirement account.
C. Mark may use his federal tax refund to purchase U.S. Series I Savings Bonds.
D. Mark may Direct Deposit his refund to his credit card account.

The answer is D. A taxpayer may not designate a credit card account for Direct Deposit of his federal tax refund. ###

9. What happens when a taxpayer has a late payment on an installment agreement?

A. The late payment will generate an automatic 30-day notice.

B. The late payment will automatically increase the statute of limitations for collecting the tax.

C. The late payment will cause the installment agreement to default.

D. The IRS will file a Notice of Deficiency.

The answer is A. A late payment on an installment agreement will generate an automatic 30-day notice. It will not cause the installment agreement to default. ###

10. Art owes more than $25,000 to the IRS. He would like to set up an installment agreement. Which of the following statements regarding his payment options is true?

A. Art may still qualify for an installment agreement, but a *Collection Information Statement*, Form 433-F, must be completed.

B. Art does not qualify for an installment agreement because he owes more than $25,000.

C. Art may still qualify for an installment agreement, but an offer in compromise must first be completed.

D. Art must enroll in EFTPS and have automatic withdrawals in order to have his installment agreement approved.

The answer is A. If a taxpayer owes more than $25,000, he may still qualify for an installment agreement, but the taxpayer will also need to complete Form 433-F, *Collection Information Statement*. ###

11. Which signature methods are acceptable for EROs to use for electronically filed returns?

A. The self-select PIN method.
B. The practitioner personal identification number method.
C. The scanned signature method.
D. Answer A and B are both correct.

The answer is D. Electronic return originators are required to use either the self-select PIN method or the practitioner personal identification number method to electronically file an individual tax return. ###

12. Which of the following tax preparers would be subject to the mandate that requires preparers to e-file their clients' returns?

A. Dean, a bookkeeper who prepares a tax return for himself.
B. Maria, an EA who only prepares payroll tax returns for her employer.
C. Scott, who files six individual tax returns and seven estate returns for compensation.
D. Chon, a CPA who files 100 returns for the Volunteer Income Tax Assistance (VITA) program.

The answer is C. Any paid preparer who files 11 or more individual or trust returns *in aggregate* in a calendar year is required to e-file. There are limited exceptions, such as for returns that cannot be e-filed (returns that require paper attachments, nonresident returns, etc.) The e-file mandate does not apply to payroll tax returns, volunteer preparers, or returns prepared under the Volunteer Income Tax Assistance (VITA) program. ###

13. Electronic Filing Identification Numbers (EFINs) are issued _____.

A. On a firm basis.
B. On a preparer basis.
C. On a client basis.
D. Only to foreign firms.

The answer is A. Electronic Filing Identification Numbers (EFINs) are issued on a firm basis. All tax return preparers in the firm are covered by a single EFIN. Providers need an EFIN to electronically file tax returns. ###

14. A Refund Anticipation Loan (RAL) is _____.

A. A refund from the Internal Revenue Service.
B. Endorsed by the Internal Revenue Service.
C. A financial product with no affiliation to the Internal Revenue Service.
D. A financial product offered by the Internal Revenue Service.

The answer is C. A Refund Anticipation Loan (RAL) is a financial product. It is not a tax refund. Instead, an RAL is a loan: money is borrowed by the taxpayer based on his anticipated tax refund. The IRS is not involved in RALs or financial products. ###

15. Which of the following is true regarding Refund Anticipating Loans?

A. Providers may compute their RAL fees using any figure from tax returns.
B. A practitioner may charge an identical flat fee to all customers applying for RALs.
C. A provider may accept a fee that is contingent upon the amount of the refund or an RAL.
D. The IRS has the responsibility for the payment of any RAL fees associated with the preparation of a return.

The answer is B. A practitioner may charge an *identical flat fee* to all customers applying for RALs, meaning the fee cannot correspond to the amount of a refund for an individual client. The practitioner must not accept a fee that is contingent upon the amount of the refund or an RAL. The IRS has no responsibility for the payment of any fees associated with the preparation of a return. ###

16. The IRS may excuse a preparer from the mandate to e-file in all of the following instances except:

A. Administrative exemptions due to technology issues.
B. An individual case of hardship documented by the preparer.
C. Lack of access to tax preparation software.
D. None of the above.

The answer is B. The IRS says it will grant e-file waivers due to hardship only on a rare, case-by-case basis, and typically only for a single year. An individual preparer's dislike of using a computer or not having appropriate software is not considered a legitimate reason to grant a hardship waiver. ###

17. Tammy is an EA who e-files a return for her client, Rick. However, Rick's e-filed return is rejected by the IRS. They cannot resolve the rejection issue, and the return must be filed on paper. In order to timely file Rick's tax return, what is the deadline for filing a paper return?

A. The due date of the return.
B. Ten calendar days after the date the IRS rejects the e-filed return.
C. Forty-eight hours after the date the IRS rejects the e-filed return.
D. Answer A and B are both correct.

The answer is D. In order to timely file a tax return, the taxpayer must file a paper return by the **later** of:

- The due date of the return; or
- Ten calendar days after the date the IRS gives notification that it rejected the e-filed return.

This is called the "Ten-Day Transmission Perfection Period," and it is additional time that the IRS gives a preparer and taxpayer to correct and resubmit a tax return without a late filing penalty. This is not an extension of time to file; rather, this is additional time that the IRS gives a preparer and taxpayer to correct and resubmit a tax return without a late filing penalty. The following steps must be followed to ensure that the paper return is identified as a *rejected electronic return* and the taxpayer is given credit for timely filing. The paper return should include the following:

- An explanation of why the paper return is being filed after the due date.
- A copy of the rejection notification.
- A brief history of actions taken to correct the electronic return. ###

18. How long must a tax practitioner retain Form 8879, *IRS e-file Signature Authorization?*

A. One year from the due date of the return or the date received by the IRS, whichever is later.
B. Two years from the due date of the return or the date received by the IRS, whichever is earlier.
C. Three years from the due date of the return or the date received by the IRS, whichever is later.
D. Three years from the due date of the return or the date received by the IRS, whichever is earlier.

The answer is C. The ERO must retain the form for three years from the due date of the return or the date received by the IRS, whichever is *later*. ###

19. Katie is an EA subject to the e-file mandate. She has power of attorney authority for her client, Timothy. What must she do to e-file Timothy's return?

A. Use Form 8453 and submit Form 2848, *Power of Attorney and Declaration of Representative,* as an attachment.
B. Use Form 8879 and submit Form 2848, *Power of Attorney and Declaration of Representative,* as an attachment.
C. Use the Practitioner PIN method as her signature requirement.
D. Katie is not allowed to e-file Timothy's return in this instance. She must file it on paper.

The answer is A. Katie must use Form 8453, *U.S. Individual Income Tax Transmittal for an IRS e-file Return*, and also submit Form 2848, *Power of Attorney and Declaration of Representative,* as an attachment. Form 8879, *IRS e-file Signature Authorization,* is used by EROs but only submitted to the IRS upon request. ###

20. The IRS may sanction providers who fail to comply with e-file regulations. It uses a specific system of categorizing how serious infractions are. Which is the most serious?

A. Level One.
B. Level Two.
C. Level Three.
D. Level Four.

The answer is C. Under the IRS system of rating e-file infractions, Level One is the less serious, Level Two is moderately serious, and Level Three is the most serious. There is no Level Four infraction. ###

21. Which individual or business is not required to e-file tax returns?

A. A partnership with 100 partners.
B. A corporation with $8 million in assets that files more than 500 information returns.
C. An EA who prepares ten Forms 1040EZ through VITA, five Forms 1040 for a small fee for neighbors, and six Forms 1041 through the tax firm she works for.
D. Both A and B.

The answer is D. A partnership with more than 100 partners must e-file. A partnership with 100 or fewer partners is not required to e-file, though it may choose to do so. A corporation with $10 million or more in assets must e-file if it files at least 250 returns. The EA in Answer C is required to e-file because she prepares 11 tax returns for compensation, which is the minimum number that triggers the e-file mandate. VITA volunteers are not covered under the e-file mandate. ###

Unit 11: IRS Documents and Pronouncements

For anyone not familiar with the IRS, the array of IRS guidance may seem puzzling at first glance. In its role of administering the tax laws enacted by Congress, the IRS must take the specifics of these laws and translate them into detailed regulations, rules, and procedures.

The IRS Office of Chief Counsel fills this crucial role by producing several kinds of documents that provide guidance to taxpayers. There are **seven** types of common IRS guidance:

1. Treasury regulations
2. Revenue rulings
3. Revenue procedures
4. Private letter rulings
5. Technical advice memorandum
6. IRS notices
7. IRS announcements

The following is a brief explanation of these forms of IRS guidance.

Treasury Regulations

Treasury regulations are the Secretary of the Treasury's interpretations of the Internal Revenue Code. The IRC authorizes the Secretary of the Treasury to "prescribe all needful rules and regulations for enforcement" of the code. All regulations are written by the Office of the Chief Counsel, IRS, and approved by the Secretary of the Treasury. Regulations are issued as interpretations of specific code sections.

The courts give weight to Treasury regulations and will generally uphold the regulations so long as the IRS's interpretation is reasonable.

> ***Note**: The IRS is bound by regulations, but the courts are not. U.S. Treasury regulations are authorized by law, but U.S. courts are not bound to follow administrative interpretations.

The courts also have the job of deciding whether a tax law challenged in court is constitutional or not.

There are three types of Treasury regulations:

- Legislative regulations
- Interpretative regulations
- Procedural regulations

Legislative Regulations

Legislative regulations are when Congress expressly delegates the authority to the Secretary or the Commissioner of the IRS to provide the requirements of a specific provision. A legislative regulation has a higher degree of authority than an interpretative regulation. A legislative regulation may be overturned if any of the following conflicts apply:

1. It is outside the power delegated to the U.S. Treasury.
2. It conflicts with a specific statute.
3. It is deemed unreasonable by the courts.

Interpretive Regulations

Interpretive regulations are issued under the IRS's general authority to interpret the IRC but are subject to challenge on the grounds that they do not reflect Congress's intent. An interpretative regulation only explains the meaning of a portion of the code. Unlike a legislative regulation, there is no grant of authority for the promulgation of an interpretative regulation by the IRS, so these regulations may be challenged.

Procedural Regulations

Procedural regulations concern the administrative provisions of the code. Procedural regulations are promulgated by the Commissioner of the IRS and not the Secretary of the Treasury. They often concern minor issues, such as when notices should be sent to employees, etc.

Proposed, Temporary, or Final?

Regulations are further classified as proposed, temporary, or final:

1. **Proposed regulations** are open to commentary from the public. Various versions of proposed regulations may be issued and withdrawn before a final regulation is made. Proposed regulations do not have authority.
2. **Temporary regulations** may remain in effect for three years, and may never be finalized.

3. **Final regulations** are issued when the regulation becomes an official Treasury decision.

Private Letter Rulings

Taxpayers who have a specific question regarding tax law may request a private letter ruling (PLR) from the IRS. A PLR is a written statement issued to a taxpayer that interprets and applies tax laws to the taxpayer's specific case. It is issued to establish tax consequences of a particular transaction before the transaction is consummated or before the taxpayer's return is filed.

A PLR is legally binding on the IRS if the taxpayer fully and accurately described the proposed transaction in the request and carries out the transaction as described. A PLR may not be relied on as precedent by other taxpayers or IRS personnel.

PLRs are made public after all the taxpayer's private, identifiable information has been redacted (the information is removed or "blacked out").

Technical Advice Memorandum

A technical advice memorandum (TAM) is written guidance furnished by the IRS Office of Chief Counsel upon the request of an IRS director, often in response to procedural questions that develop during an audit.

A TAM is issued in response to a technical or procedural question that develops during:

- The examination of a taxpayer's return
- Consideration of a taxpayer's claim for refund or credit
- A request for a determination letter
- Processing and considering non-docketed cases in an appeals office

Technical advice memoranda are issued only on closed transactions and provide the interpretation of proper application of tax laws, tax treaties, regulations, revenue rulings, or other precedents.

The advice rendered represents the position of the IRS, but only relates to the specific case in question. Technical advice memoranda are made public after all information has been removed that could identify the taxpayer whose circumstances triggered a specific memorandum.

241

Revenue Rulings and Revenue Procedures

The IRS issues both revenue rulings and revenue procedures for the information and guidance of taxpayers. Neither has the force of Treasury Department regulations, but they may be used as precedents.

A *revenue ruling* typically states the IRS position, while a *revenue procedure* provides instructions concerning that position.

Revenue Rulings

Revenue rulings are intended to promote uniform application of the IRC. The national office of the IRS issues revenue rulings, which are published in issues of the Internal Revenue Bulletin and the Federal Register. A revenue ruling is not binding in Tax Court or any other U.S. court. However, revenue rulings can be used to avoid certain IRS penalties.

The numbering system for revenue rulings corresponds to the year in which they are issued. Thus, for example, revenue ruling 80-20 was the twentieth revenue ruling issued in 1980.

Revenue Procedures

Revenue procedures are official IRS statements of procedure that affect the rights or duties of taxpayers or other members of the public under the IRC and related statutes or information that, although not necessarily affecting the rights of the public, should be a matter of public knowledge. A revenue procedure may be cited as precedent, but it does not have the force of law.

> **Example:** A *revenue ruling* will announce that taxpayers may deduct certain automobile expenses. The *revenue procedure* will then explain how taxpayers must deduct, allocate, or compute these automobile expenses.

IRS Notices

An official IRS notice is a public pronouncement that may contain guidance involving substantive interpretations of the IRC or other provisions of the law. Information that is commonly published in IRS notices includes:

- Weighted average interest rate updates
- Inflation adjustment factors
- Changes to IRS regulations
- Presidentially Declared Disaster Areas

- IRS requests for public comments on changes to regulations, rulings, or procedures

IRS Announcements

An IRS announcement is a public pronouncement that has only immediate or short-term value.

For example, announcements can be used to summarize regulations without making any substantive interpretation; to state what regulations will say when they are certain to be published in the immediate future; or to notify taxpayers of an approaching deadline.

Some examples of IRS announcements include:

- Availability of new or corrected IRS forms or publications
- Updated standard mileage rates
- Announcement of an IRS settlement program
- Correction of a typographical error in a previously published revenue ruling or revenue procedure

Freedom of Information Act Requests (FOIA)

The Freedom of Information Act (FOIA) is a law designed to ensure public access to U.S. government records. Upon written request, agencies of the U.S. government, including the IRS, are required to disclose requested records, unless they can be withheld under certain exemptions in the FOIA.

The FOIA applies to records created by federal agencies and does not cover records held by Congress, the courts, or state and local government agencies. Each state has its own public access laws.

Reasons Records May be Denied Under the FOIA

The IRS may withhold an IRS record that falls under one of the FOIA's exemptions or exclusions. The exemptions protect against the disclosure of information that would harm the following: national security, the privacy of individuals, the proprietary interests of business, the functioning of the government, and other important recognized interests.

When a record contains some information that qualifies as exempt, the entire record is not necessarily exempt. Instead, the FOIA specifically provides that any portions of a record that can be set apart must be provided to a requester after deletion of the exempt portions.

Whenever a FOIA request is denied, the IRS must give the reason for denial and explain the right to appeal to the head of the agency. A taxpayer may contest the type or amount of fees that were charged in the processing of the records request. A taxpayer also may appeal any other type of adverse determination under the FOIA, such as the failure of the IRS to conduct an adequate search for requested documents. However, a taxpayer may not file an administrative appeal for the lack of a timely response by the IRS.

A person whose request was granted in part and denied in part may appeal the part that was denied. If the IRS has agreed to disclose some but not all of the requested documents, the filing of an appeal does not affect the release of the documents that can be disclosed. There is no charge for filing an FOIA appeal.

Unit 11: Questions

1. Which of the following statements regarding revenue rulings is correct?

A. Revenue rulings CANNOT be used to avoid certain IRS penalties.
B. Revenue rulings CAN be used to avoid certain IRS penalties.
C. Revenue rulings are not official IRS guidance.
D. None of the above.

The answer is B. Revenue rulings CAN be used to avoid certain IRS penalties. Taxpayers may rely on revenue rulings as official IRS guidance on an issue to make a decision regarding taxable income, deductions, and also how to avoid certain IRS penalties. ###

2. What is a private letter ruling?

A. It is a private letter that a taxpayer writes to the IRS.
B. It is a private letter issued by the U.S. Tax Court.
C. It is a request by a taxpayer to the IRS to rule about a particular tax matter.
D. It is a request by the IRS to Congress about tax issues.

The answer is C. A private letter ruling is initiated by a taxpayer who has a question about a particular transaction. A taxpayer may request a PLR from the IRS. It cannot be used as a precedent by other taxpayers or the IRS. ###

3. Which is not a type of official IRS guidance?

A. Treasury regulation.
B. Private letter ruling.
C. Technical advice memorandum.
D. Tax Court memorandum opinion.

The answer is D. A Tax Court memorandum opinion is a pronouncement of the Tax Court and not of the IRS. ###

4. Which of the following statements regarding the legality of revenue rulings and revenue procedures is correct?

A. Revenue rulings are binding in court, but revenue procedures are not.
B. Revenue rulings and revenue procedures are binding in court.
C. Revenue rulings and revenue procedures are not binding in court.
D. Revenue rulings and revenue procedures are binding in Tax Court, but not in U.S. District Courts.

The answer is C. Revenue rulings and revenue procedures are not binding in Tax Court or any other court. However, taxpayers may use revenue rulings and revenue procedures as official IRS guidance. ###

5. Which of the following choices is not a type of Treasury regulation?

A. Supporting regulation.
B. Interpretative regulation.
C. Legislative regulation.
D. Procedural regulation.

The answer is A. There are three types of Treasury regulations: legislative, interpretive, and procedural. There is no such thing as a "supporting regulation."###

6. A legislative regulation has a higher degree of authority than _____.

A. The Internal Revenue Code.
B. A Supreme Court decision.
C. An interpretative regulation.
D. None of the above.

The answer is C. A legislative regulation has a higher degree of authority than an interpretative regulation. ###

7. When a Treasury regulation becomes "official," what happens?

A. A procedural regulation is issued.
B. A final regulation is issued.
C. A temporary regulation is issued.
D. A Tax Court memorandum is published.

The answer is B. A final regulation is issued when a Treasury regulation becomes an official Treasury decision. ###

8. A private letter ruling is *legally binding* on the IRS if _____.

A. The taxpayer fully and accurately described the proposed transaction in the request and carries out the transaction as described.
B. The IRS is notified of any discrepancies on a taxpayer's return.
C. The taxpayer goes to the Tax Court and requests a formal decision.
D. None of the above.

The answer is A. A PLR is binding on the IRS if the taxpayer fully and accurately described the proposed transaction in the request and carries out the transaction as described. A PLR may not be relied on as precedent by other taxpayers or IRS personnel. ###

9. Which has the highest level of authority?

A. Revenue ruling.
B. Procedural regulation.
C. Interpretative regulation.
D. Legislative regulation.

The answer is D. A legislative regulation is authorized by Congress to provide the material requirements of a specific IRC provision. If written correctly, a legislative regulation carries the same authority as the IRC itself. It can only be overturned if it is outside the power delegated to the U.S. Treasury; it conflicts with a specific statute; or it is deemed unreasonable by the courts. ###

Index

I

J

K

L

M

N

O

P

W

Also Available from PassKey Publications

The Enrolled Agent Tax Consulting Practice Guide:
Learn How to Develop, Market, and Operate a Profitable Tax and IRS Representation Practice

ISBN-13: 978-0982266045
Available in Kindle and Nook editions and as a paperback

About the Authors

Collette Szymborski is a certified public accountant and the managing partner of Elk Grove CPA Accountancy Corporation. She specializes in the taxation of corporations, individuals, and exempt entities. Elk Grove CPA also does estate planning.

Richard Gramkow is an enrolled agent with more than sixteen years of experience in various areas of taxation. He holds a master's degree in taxation from Rutgers University and is currently a tax manager for a publicly held Fortune 500 company in the New York metropolitan area.

Christy Pinheiro is an enrolled agent, registered tax return preparer, Accredited Business Accountant, and writer. Christy was an accountant for two private CPA firms and for the State of California before going into private practice. She is a member of the California Society of Enrolled Agents and CalCPA.